The Rise and Fall of the
POLICE BOX

About the Author

John 'Jack' Bunker served as a Metropolitan Police officer for thirty-six years in various divisions in central and north-west London retiring in the rank of Superintendent at New Scotland Yard. As a keen researcher on the history of police communications this is a follow up to his previous book *From Rattle to Radio* published in 1988. John is a member of *The Police History Society* where all aspects of police history are encouraged at any level.

Front cover images: Courtesy of the Metropolitan Police and Yorkshire Regional Newspapers Ltd.

Rear cover images: Left: Police kiosk at Avoncroft Museum of Buildings (Author's image). Middle: Police kiosk outside Sheffield Town Hall (Courtesy of Peter Mitchell). Right: PC Dennis 'Tug' Wilson outside a Police box in Nottingham (ownership of image unknown).

The Rise and Fall of the
POLICE BOX

John Bunker

BREWIN BOOKS

First published by
Brewin Books Ltd, 56 Alcester Road,
Studley, Warwickshire B80 7LG in 2011

www.brewinbooks.com

Reprinted September 2014

ISBN: 978-1-85858-465-2

A Cataloguing in Publication Record
for this title is available from the British Library.

Typeset in Bembo
Printed in Great Britain by
CMP Digital Print Solutions.

CONTENTS

ACKNOWLEDGEMENTS

The author is grateful for the assistance given in the preparation of this book by the staff of the Beamish Museum Photo Archive; British Newspaper Library, Colindale; British Telecom Archive, High Holborn, British Telecom Showcase, Blackfriars (now closed); East Sussex Record Office; Glamorgan Record Office; France Telecom, Paris; Historic Scotland, Edinburgh; Hull City Archives; Leicestershire Record Office; Metropolitan Police Archives; Mitchell Library, Glasgow; National Archives, Kew; Northamptonshire Constabulary; North Yorkshire Police; Plymouth City Museum; Post Office Archives, St Martins le Grand; Siemens Museum, Munich; Science Museum Library; Strathclyde Police; Walsall Local History Centre.

Particularly appreciated are the individuals who gave their time and assistance – Roger Appleby and Ray Hayter City of London Police Museum; Maggie Bird, Robin Gilles, Ray Seal and Ken Stone, Metropolitan Police Museum Collection; Mr E. Birch, British Telecom Museum, Oxford (now closed); Duncan Broady, Greater Manchester Police Museum; Alastair Dinsmor, Glasgow Police Museum; John Endicott, Kent Police Museum; Brian Estill, Devon and Cornwall Police Museum; Mr T. E. J. Howells, Gwent Constabulary Museum; Ralph Lindley, Ripon Museum Trust; Geoff Marston, Grampian Police Museum; John Mason, Norfolk Constabulary Archives; Tony Rose, Coventry Police Museum; Barbara Hick and Chief Superintendent B. Ledgard West Yorkshire Police Media and Public Relations Department; Tony Mossman, Merseyside Police Press and Publicity Officer; Pat Percival, Northamptonshire Police; Jeff Cowdell and Alf Tunstall, Staffordshire Police historians; Jim Cramer, Hampshire Constabulary historian; Bob Dobson, Lancashire Constabulary historian; Terry Gardner, Warwickshire Police historian; Thomas Madigan, Luton Borough Police historian; Bob Pooler, Worcestershire Constabulary historian; Constable John Bryson, Metropolitan Police Communications Branch; Sergeant Richard Farmery, Metropolitan Police Training School Hendon; Mr J. W. Hoch and Sergeant Willie MacFarlane, Tayside Police; Chief Superintendent Ian MacPherson and Eddie McMillan, Lothian and Borders Police; Andy Reid, Royal Parks Constabulary; Bob Richards and David Storer Nottinghamshire Police; Chief Superintendent Tuckwood, Leicestershire Constabulary; Superintendent Les Walters, Cambridgeshire Constabulary; Paul Dixon, retired West Yorkshire Police; Ian Ewence, retired Surrey Police; Fred Feather, retired Essex Police; Sean Hollands, retired Kent

Police; Keith Rigg, retired Sussex Police; Mike Collings, retired Metropolitan Police previously Northampton Police; Mr S. F. Spice, NARPO (Kent); Paul Gibson's collection of Hull pictures; Christopher Ketchell, Hull College; Alan Hayhurst, Police History Society; Rodney Marshall, Telecommunications Heritage Group; Harry Wynne, North Eastern Police History Society; photographic assistance by Jean Bunker, Bob Flashman, Sidney Galloway, Eddie Gleeson, Martin Holmes, Peter Keasley, Peter Mitchell, Emma McLean and Lucinda James. Many others gave assistance and apologies are tendered for any names that are omitted.

Thanks also to those retired officers who gave the benefit of their experiences with police boxes, although not all could be included in this book.

Chapter 1

INTRODUCTION

O rganised policing in Great Britain was marked by the formation of the Metropolitan Police force in September 1829. Subsequent legislation either authorised or compelled other cities, boroughs and counties to follow London's lead until a patchwork of forces, ranging widely in territorial area and population, covered the whole of the nation. The absorbing of borough forces into the county constabularies or large city forces, at various times throughout the nineteenth century, continued well into the second half of the twentieth. The 1974/5 amalgamations, linking some counties for policing purposes, have now left England and Wales with forty-three separate forces, Scotland with a further eight and the single Police Service of Northern Ireland (previously the Royal Ulster Constabulary). This does not take account of those organisations, such as the British Transport Police, the Civil Nuclear Constabulary (previously the United Kingdom Atomic Energy Authority Constabulary) and the Ministry of Defence Police, with their own special policing responsibilities.

Territorial divisions, each with their own central or divisional headquarters station, have provided the structure for efficient operational management of force areas since the earliest days. The sectioning of the larger divisions into a series of sub-divisions, with their own headquarters stations and often additional satellite offices, gave residents reasonable access to their local police force. It is the beat, however, patrolled by the constable, that has provided the protection and reassurance the public need, although in recent years the motorcar has become a more important feature of policing.

Both the constable and the public were seriously disadvantaged in the early days by the lack of communication. In order to prevent crime and provide the best service to the residents of an area strict instructions, particularly in urban locations, as to how the officer should patrol the whole of his beat were necessary. Rules in some forces even laid down the speed at which the constable should actually walk his beat. Formal patrolling meant that any resident requiring the services of a constable merely remained in one spot on the street and, in theory, within a relatively short time, a policeman should pass. Often, however, the only answer was to visit the police station in person.

As areas became more built-up and congested the guarantee that a constable would regularly pass through all parts of his beat became impossible to achieve. To overcome this weakness fixed points were often introduced at strategic locations where a constable would be constantly available, at all or particular times of the day, to give assistance to the public when required. In time some of these fixed points were provided with a shelter for the constable. Eventually police boxes, in the form of kiosks, street pillars or wall units, connected to a police station, provided that missing communication link, which the new policing systems needed to operate more effectively.

The origins of police box systems go back to the street alarm or call points, available towards the end of the nineteenth century, albeit restricted to a few large towns and cities. The heyday of the police telephone kiosk and pillar were the decades between the 1920s and 1960s when a greater proportion of the city, county borough and borough forces, and to a lesser extent county constabularies, introduced organised systems to meet the needs of their own particular areas. Generally both policeman and public benefited from having access to the facility and, no doubt, the schemes played their part in improving the public's relations with the police. The force amalgamations and reorganisations of the late 1960s coincided with the introduction of the personal radio as a feature of the constable's equipment giving him that immediate contact, from all parts of his beat, that the police box could not provide.

The private subscriber telephone, installed in more and more households, and the public telephone kiosk, which had been previously available on a more limited scale, provided ready access to the police. The '999' service had become an established method of contacting the police in an emergency. The eventual decline of the police box and pillar was rapid although, in some forces where a specific need existed, they survived for some years. Few remnants of previously flourishing systems can now be found; even those boxes that exist are often in poor condition or in use for other purposes.

In the 1920s police box schemes, in many cases, provided the substitute for police stations that had to be closed within a force area to make financial savings. Press reports in October 2011, announced that one in three of the now much diminished number of police stations throughout the country could be closed to the public, thereby allowing chief constables today to direct their reduced financial resources effectively towards front line policing. This time it will not be the police box that comes to the rescue but the innovative development of the internet, social media and non-emergency telephone contact (now with the further benefits of mobile phones) as an addition to the '999' service. There will also be a case for setting up police counters, relatively cheaply, in civic buildings like libraries and leisure centres, supported by Neighbourhood Policing Teams.

As a police constable using the police boxes and posts in London in the 1950s and 1960s I cannot say that they are remembered with any great affection. A dirty, damp and cold concrete kiosk is not a particularly inviting place on a winter's night or at any other time come to that. I preferred to be walking the streets. My recollections are of dashing to the box in an attempt to make the scheduled 'ring' on time or to respond to the flashing light indicating that the station wanted to make contact. My unofficial endeavours to study for promotion in the police box were usually abandoned due to the discomfort.

With research covering the whole of the United Kingdom it is often difficult to establish which police forces adopted street communication systems and when. Sometimes Post Office, police and other public records, along with fading memories, appear contradictory. Many records have been destroyed during amalgamations or have not been readily available although, had time allowed searches at County Record Offices throughout the country for Watch Committee Minutes and similar documents to be made, an even more complete picture may have been possible. Reference has been made to systems used in other countries, particularly the United States of America, as these often had an influence here. Hopefully the cross-section of systems and equipment covered in this book will provide an accurate and interesting account, and be useful to future researchers. The author accepts responsibility for any errors or omissions that occur.

An important landmark in policing, now almost entirely passed, is documented in the book drawing, in places, on the memories of constables who took the police box for granted in pursuit of their day-to-day duties. Describing in detail the major phases in the development of systems throughout the country, judgements are not generally made on their success or otherwise. Neither is it intended to describe the more technical details of the associated communications systems. Surely the 'Tardis' of the *Doctor Who* television series will not remain the only lasting memory of a system that provided reassurance to the residents of the towns and cities of this country for almost fifty years.

Chapter 2

THE PURPOSE OF THE
POLICE BOX SYSTEM

Police telephone kiosks and other street call points were a feature of policing in only a few major towns and cities at the close of the nineteenth century and during the early years of the twentieth. Some initial installations, where they failed to entirely meet the needs of the police, did not progress beyond an experimental phase. Liverpool and Glasgow were two notable successes where substantial systems operated at the end of the nineteenth century.

Sunderland County Borough Police pioneered, in 1923, the modern integrated police box system soon imitated by other forces throughout the country. Although sometimes constrained by insufficient funds each force would, as far as possible, tailor a system to meet their own individual needs; for example the requirements in a busy built-up city would be different to those in a rural location. The financial savings that boxes made possible, through reductions in the number of police buildings and manpower, came at the top of the agenda for many in authority lending support to this new system of policing. Improved communication with those on the streets, using the latest technology of the day, formed the priority as far as the operational policeman and the public were concerned.

Police box systems generally permitted chief constables to substantially reduce the number of police stations by replacing them with a network of street kiosks. These structures, in effect, almost became 'mini-police stations'. Policemen, required previously for administrative duties in the closed stations, could be diverted to patrolling the streets or, alternatively, the established numbers of personnel reduced. Reducing police buildings meant substantial savings in the maintenance of the many that were old and costly to run. Police stations (like the beats) required supervisory ranks on duty; with fewer stations reductions in the number of inspectors and sergeants were sometimes possible. In some forces, where previously sparsely inhabited areas were becoming more built-up, the introduction of a police box system allowed the policing of these more highly populated places without increasing the numbers of officers required to achieve this.

People in this country had greater expectations of their police by the 1920s; crimes were increasing, particularly those involving the motorcar. The police box, strategically located, could provide that reassurance demanded in residential areas where public use of the telephone link with the police station was actively encouraged. Some argued that the public were more likely to give information to the police if they could do so using the free facility offered by a police box, rather than going to the police station or using a public telephone. A minority of forces did, however, resist allowing general access to the new facility.

In many forces a police box system made possible a substantial increase in the patrolling time of the constable achieved by abandoning the need for him to attend the police station, at the commencement of his tour of duty, to receive instructions prior to walking out to his beat. Everything could be accomplished through the direct telephone line between either the divisional station or the force headquarters, and the kiosk. The constable even took his meal in the box, provided, in some places, with a cooker. At the end of his duty he 'booked off' from the box before going home; in fact, with no time spent walking to and from the beat, it was covered at all times.

Sales publicity showing AJS motorcycles used in conjunction with police boxes.

Some forces retained the long-standing procedure where officers paraded on and off duty at the police station even after police boxes had been introduced. Notably the Metropolitan Police considered that the advantage gained, through proper prior briefing and inspection of constables by the sergeant, outweighed the benefits of any extra time on the beat. Subsequently a number of other forces did revert to this system.

Where constables spent their whole duty time on the beat nominated police boxes were supplied regularly with current force instructions, information relating to crimes and other printed matter; this information would previously have been read to the constable, or studied by him, during parade time at the police station. Where beats were covered by cycle patrols storage for the bicycles was often available within the box or adjacent to it.

Many chief constables abandoned the rigid timetables for patrolling beats where, during his patrol, the constable was expected to make a number of scheduled 'meets' with the sergeant. Although supervision could not be compromised, introduction of a system of 'discretionary patrol' allowed the constable to cover his beat in a way that more accurately matched the needs of the particular area. The police box in effect maintained the supervision through the constable 'ringing in' to his station or headquarters at specified times during his tour of duty. These 'rings', usually recorded by the constable in a logbook kept at the box, were noted at the station for checking by supervisors. Not only did this ensure that the officer worked his beat correctly, but also that he had not fallen foul of any trouble.

Police box systems were designed to improve the response to incidents and crimes requiring police attendance, bearing in mind that their introduction preceded the '999' emergency telephone system by many years. An effective response to any calls for assistance from the boxes relied upon transport, by way of either motorcycle combinations, motorcars or vans, albeit initially without the luxury of wireless communication on the vehicles. (The police use of wireless was at an experimental stage in a few forces during the 1920s.) The box provided the most

Metropolitan Police Constable calling in from the Police Box. Credit: Metropolitan Police.

First Aid at the Police Box. Credit: Metropolitan Police.

Ringing in from the Police Post – Metropolitan Police. Credit: Metropolitan Police.

efficient means available at the time for disseminating information and, accompanied by adequate transport, was seen as a way of reducing crime. In fact such was the concern about the increase in 'motor bandit crimes' that, in 1927, His Majesty's Inspector of Constabulary, Sir L.W. Atcherley, visited Sunderland to consider the impact of the police box system in this respect. Whether these systems actually had much impact on reducing crime levels is a matter for debate.

Regular telephonic communication with the station meant that routine messages, requiring action on the beat, could be passed to and from the constable during his tour of duty thereby improving efficiency. Information concerning crimes that had occurred since the officers had come on duty could be disseminated quickly from headquarters. In earlier times, where important information had to be given to the man on the beat, messengers would have been sent out on foot or pedal cycle to find him.

Albeit used to a much lesser extent by them, the police box gave C.I.D. detectives and plain-clothes officers valuable communication with the station when they were in need of information. Senior officers also benefited from these improved links with their headquarters from the street.

The majority of police box systems incorporated a signal facility, usually a flashing light, to alert the constable to the box to receive a message from his station. These signals, when operated on all boxes on the division, also provided an effective method of rapidly mobilising a force of constables to deal with a major emergency. Officers could be instructed to remain at their respective boxes until collected by a police car, or they could be directed to make their way immediately to the location of the emergency.

The direct telephone line, in many cases used to call for an ambulance or the fire brigade, allowed earlier street alarm systems to be abandoned. First aid equipment, kept in the kiosks or posts, met the demands posed by the increasing number of road accidents.

Pending the arrival of transport the police box provided, in an emergency, temporary accommodation to hold an arrested person. Walking prisoners for long distances through the streets could, to some extent, be avoided. During wartime air raid sirens were operated from many boxes.

Later years saw the growth of pillars, as an alternative to kiosks in congested urban areas, albeit with less facilities than the latter could provide.

Undoubtedly police box systems had considerable impact on policing in this country. They allowed better use of expensive manpower and, in many areas, fewer police stations were actually required to cover larger and more densely populated divisions. Much of the previous work of the police station could be handled on the beat by use of efficient communication. As Frederick Crawley, then Chief Constable of Newcastle, was to observe in 1929 in relation to the importance of police box schemes, 'Still in 1923 all forces were truly pantomimic in their organisation as compared with today's policing in an up to date force.'

Chapter 3

THE DEVELOPMENT OF
STREET CALL POINTS (1880-c.1926)

A series of detached and unsupported outposts' *(Siemens Sales Catalogue)* gives an accurate picture of the men on the beats in those far-off days of the nineteenth century. Each constable provided his service to the residents of the beat in almost complete isolation from the police station and colleagues, apart from scheduled meetings with the sergeant. When in trouble he could, of course, resort to his rattle or whistle, or even shine his lantern in the direction in which another officer may be patrolling, in the hope that his 'cry' for help would be acted upon.

The beat's resident shared similar isolation from those employed to protect him having to shout for help or perhaps using a rattle of his own to summon the constable. He could, of course, set out for the police station on foot, horseback or cab and may, by chance, meet a policeman on the way. Perhaps if he remained where he was the man on the beat would pass by. Perhaps! Not a very reassuring state of affairs.

Although the electric telegraph was operating publicly in Britain in the early 1840s, many years were to elapse before police forces introduced their own internal equipment for communication between divisional stations and the force headquarters. Not until 1867 did the Metropolitan Police, for example, install its permanent internal network of ABC telegraph machines. These early telegraph facilities did not, however, incorporate any communication with the constable on the beat.

As early as 1874 the Electric Telegraph Company was offering householders a telegraphic call point system giving its subscribers a service through a company call station. The claim was that at the press of a button by the subscriber at his home, 'a messenger, cab or policeman' could be summoned. Although it is unclear whether or not the facility was a success it did actually contain the rudiments of that which the police would use in their street facilities over a decade later.

Alarm, signalling or call points, in the form of small cupboard style boxes containing the communication equipment, and supported on pillars, lampposts or fixed to walls, were the earliest form of police communication from the street. Preceding this development fire brigades (in many parts of this country under police control) were already operating street alarms widely. Situated in prominent locations throughout a city or town the public (or police) could alert firemen to a fire. For example, the Glasgow Fire Brigade introduced a system of eighty-two alarms across the city in 1878 and London's Metropolitan Fire Brigade (not associated with the Metropolitan Police) was another early user of a system. In 1880, fire stations at Westminster, Clerkenwell, Whitechapel, Kennington Lane and Southwark were connected to forty street call points, which had been increased to three hundred some six years later.

By 1852 fire alarms had been introduced in Boston in the United States. The 1880s saw police forces in the larger towns and cities in America, where considerable experience had by then been gained with the fire alarms, pioneering the concept of communication between the police station and the officer on the street, with Washington DC one of the first in 1883. The Commissioner of Boston described his force's facility (introduced in 1886 and known as the Wilson Public Safety System) as 'The most valuable improvement that has so far been introduced into the Police Department'. This view echoed that of other police chiefs across America. Police in Toronto, Canada, were operating sixty street call points in 1888, incorporating a gong, flashing signal light and telephone. In Europe by the 1880s alarm systems, with telephone connections, appeared on the streets in Paris.

Success in their own country led inventors and companies from America to promote their equipment in Great Britain with attractive offers to pay for installation, along with the other costs of a trial, anticipating that this would result in a subsequent lucrative force-wide contract. It seems that the Commissioner of the Metropolis, Charles Warren, was the first to take up such an offer that resulted in nine iron call boxes, invented by an American, William Rust, being positioned on the streets of Islington on 25th March 1888. Rust's boxes, supplied by the Public Safety Signal Association and measuring 21 inches by 14 inches by 6 inches, were supported on wooden platforms, whereas permanent sites in America would have found them fixed to walls. Direct wires connected the boxes with the transmitting/receiving apparatus at Islington Police Station.

These early systems usually incorporated many complex features. The constable on his Islington beat opened the box with a personal key, and could send messages to the station that were received there on timed paper slips. In urgent cases he could cause a bell to be activated at the station alerting the officer on duty there to speak to him on the telephone. Unfortunately the telephone signals were often poor.

The officer on the beat was alerted to a call transmitted from the station by a bell sounding at the call point. Unlike a visual signal, which could have been seen from some distance, the bell was often not heard by the constable patrolling the noisy streets of north London. Promises by the inventor to design a visual indicator never materialised.

The inventor not only paid for the installation but, additionally, met the cost of a horse, wagon (with stretcher) and civilian driver, retained at Islington Police Station between 3 p.m. and 1 a.m. the next day. This transport was sent out on receipt of a call for assistance made from the box. During 1889, 1890 and up until July 1891 the wagon was used to convey a total of 1209 prisoners for offences ranging from felonies to drunkenness. The wagon also ensured that the constable would be back on his beat sooner after he had made an arrest.

The residents of Islington were delighted with the call points as many had been supplied with keys allowing them to send a signal direct to the police station in an emergency (once inserted the key could not be removed except by a police officer). In fact, in 1889, the ratepayers of the Parish of St Mary petitioned for the facility to be retained permanently. They praised it as 'a great additional protection to the district' adding that, 'the Police Force has been materially aided in the prevention of crime and the detection and capture of criminals'. They went on to explain, 'that the knowledge of the rapidity with which aid can be summoned, and descriptions of the criminal distributed throughout the district, does exercise a strongly deterrent effect upon the criminal classes'. The inspectors at Islington supported this view, also emphasising the confidence the system provided to their constables knowing that assistance could be readily obtained by using the box if they were in trouble. The matter was even raised in Parliament in July when the Home Secretary was asked whether he intended to support the general adoption of a police signal system. He evaded the matter stating that it was still under consideration.

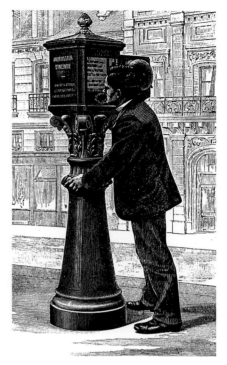

Street call points in Paris, 1893. Credit: France Telecom.

The Metropolitan Police continued to maintain the system after the initial free evaluation period – at a cost of £349.0s.1d. and £388.19s.4d. for the financial years 1890/91 and 1891/92. Favourable petitioning and praises did not, however, encourage the Commissioner to support a permanent force-wide network of boxes. Consideration was given at one stage to increasing the number of boxes to twenty-five, using a more efficient radial system of wires, at a cost of £365.5s. (it did not include the cost of the wagon, etc.); this was not pursued.

Adverse comments about the bell, the lack of a visual signal and the poor telephone communication during the trial, influenced the decision not to extend it further, although there is little doubt that finance was the major factor. An extension of the system would have been very costly; even Superintendent Sherlock, the officer in charge of 'N' Division, indicated that he found no saving to police funds during the experiment at Islington Sub-Division. He did, however, recognise the potential for improved supervision if constables were instructed to 'report in' from a call point at scheduled times during a tour of duty. This may, of course, have led to a reduction in the number of sergeants required for supervision.

By August 1892 the horse and wagon had been withdrawn and a recommendation made that a cab should be hired instead as and when required. Although Rust, who had returned to America, asked that police continue to use his boxes, free of charge, they were soon neglected and fell into a bad state of repair. Removal from the streets of Islington in early 1894 saw an end to north London's attempt at street communication.

Toronto Police Pillar c. 1890, Toronto Police Museum, Canada.

Offers to the Metropolitan Police of call point systems continued during the period that the Islington boxes were in operation. (It is, however, often difficult to ascertain whether or not systems, bearing different names, were, in fact, identical having been taken over by another company.) An invention by Brewer and Smith, which incorporated a visual signalling device, was drawn to the attention of the Commissioner by the suppliers, the American Trading Company, early in 1888. Some three years later Frank Stuart of Twickenham sought authority to install his suitably converted fire alarms, free of charge, at selected sites in the West End of London. These offers were declined.

James Monro, Commissioner of Police 1888-1890. Credit: Metropolitan Police.

In March 1890, the Westminster Palace Hotel in London hosted a display of the Morgan's Automatic Police Signalling System in which the suppliers, the National Signal Company, had for some time been keen to interest the Metropolitan Police. The superintendents of the force attended and generally reported favourably on what they saw. The Commissioner, James Monro, however, was not inclined to install another system whilst the Islington boxes were under evaluation. Rust, the inventor of the existing facility, thought that a simultaneous trial would allow a fair comparison between his and the proposed system.

The chairman of the National Signal Company, Otto Friederici, expounded on the benefits to police of the Morgan's system observing that without it the constable was 'at the mercy of marauders, burglars or riotous mobs, and to call for assistance he must have resource to a whistle or rattle, summoning assistance if lucky, otherwise giving loud and timely notice to perhaps the very men he wishes to surprise'.

Finally the Home Office gave approval for the experiment to go ahead and, in March 1892, ten street lampposts housing the facility went into operational service at selected junctions on the streets of Brixton and Clapham. Sites were selected so that the maximum number of patrolling constables could see the call points. Difficulty experienced by the Post Office with wayleaves had been partially responsible for the delay in installation. As usual the supplier met the initial costs.

From the central apparatus, located at Brixton Police Station, of this even more complex system, the man on the beat could be summoned to the post by the operator

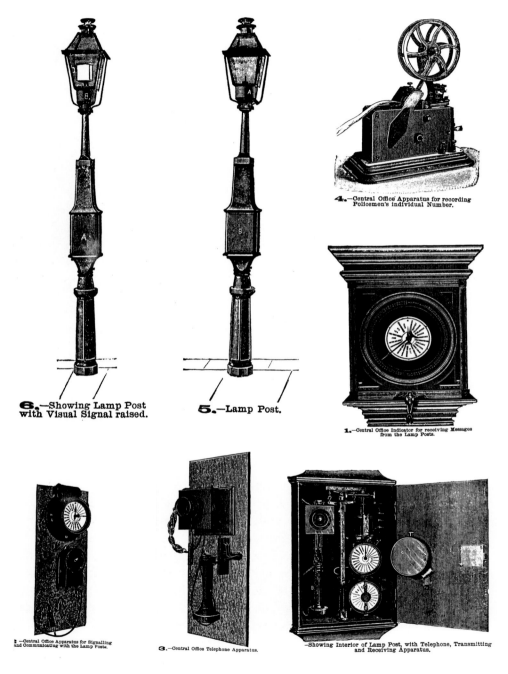

4.—Central Office Apparatus for recording Policemen's individual Number.

6.—Showing Lamp Post with Visual Signal raised.

5.—Lamp Post.

1.—Central Office Indicator for receiving Messages from the Lamp Posts.

2.—Central Office Apparatus for Signalling and Communicating with the Lamp Posts.

3.—Central Office Telephone Apparatus.

—Showing Interior of Lamp Post, with Telephone, Transmitting and Receiving Apparatus.

Police call point system installed in Brixton 1892.

remotely changing the colour of its lamp to red. In response to the light signal the constable would open the cupboard set into the lamppost with his personal key. Inside a pointer on a receiving dial indicated one of a series of standard instructions, sent from the station, to which he would react. Although generally relying on these messages a telephone link to the station was available as an alternative. Before leaving the box the constable extinguished the red light with a metal rod.

A need for assistance at the post required the constable to move a pointer on a dial to one of a series of preformatted messages, such as 'wagon wanted' or 'send officer', depending upon the extent of the problem. His request would appear on a receiving dial at the station and the appropriate resources sent to his aid. A facility existed for a Morse receiver to be activated by use of an instrument carried by a constable and inserted into the transmitting equipment at the lamppost. Whether all the features were actually used during the trial is unclear.

'Citizen' keys were available for residents which, when inserted into a lock on the post, set off a signal at the station, and could not be removed except by a policeman. Such a call from a member of the public would cause the officer at the police station to activate the red light to alert the man on the beat.

A comparison between the Islington and Brixton systems did indicate that the latter was more suitable, but the Commissioner decided that neither provided a substantial improvement to efficiency or financial benefits to the force.

Siemens Brothers Ltd. took over the National Signal Company's system in early 1893 only to be informed of the Commissioner's decision not to adopt it on a permanent basis. Mr Siemens asked for the facility to remain in place for a period of time and referred to the 'satisfactory' Brixton trial in the company's sales brochure. Apart from a few minor changes it does seem that Siemens retained the majority of the originally designed features.

The Metropolitan Police decided to consult independent engineers, Campbell Swinton, for advice on the way forward with street communication. The recommendation from the consultants was that the force should decide exactly what they required from a system, and have it manufactured to their own specification without being unduly influenced by companies trying to promote their own products. The police telephone kiosk seemed to meet the needs of the Metropolitan Police in preference to the pillar, and subsequent offers of Gamewell's Police Alarms and the Davis Signal System were declined.

Whereas the Metropolitan Police were rather sceptical about the value of street communication the Head Constable of Liverpool City Police, John W. Nott-Bower, was more progressive in his views and, as early as 1887, was telling his Watch Committee of the advantages of accepting the Public Safety Signal Association's system in the city. (This appears to be the system subsequently installed in Islington and described above.)

At this time the Committee decided against the recommendation due to the high cost and the undesirability of laying overhead and underground wires to the call points.

Nott-Bower did not give up and, a few years later, arranged for Liverpool's Engineer, H. P. Boulnois, to visit and examine the facility being installed at Brixton. He was most impressed and in March 1892 sought to introduce a facility in the city on the grounds of 'efficiency and economy'. Although the Brixton system was considered, Liverpool initially opted for a trial of Edward Davis's Police Signal System consisting of metal wall boxes containing the communication apparatus.

The National Telephone Company undertook a full trial in 1896 of a system (probably Davis's) whereby the constable opened the box with an individualised key and inside he pulled one of a series of knobs depending upon the service he required – fire brigade, ambulance, wagon wanted, etc. – that was relayed to the receiving apparatus at the headquarters. The time of receipt of the message and the identity of the box from which it emanated were automatically recorded on paper tape at the central station. A small visual indicator on the street box could be changed from red to white to signify a call from the headquarters. To answer this call the man on the beat would use the telephone. Each constable was issued with a 'report key' used to send a signal to the station that he had visited a box on his beat.

Liverpool's city police stations were already connected by telephone to the Dale Street central police office when the successful trial,

John Nott-Bower, Chief Constable, Liverpool City Police, 1881-1902. Credit: Merseyside Police.

Liverpool City Police call point system. Credit: Merseyside Police.

with ten call points, was completed. The National Telephone Company provided the contract estimated at £2,458 annually for the installation of a total of 257 boxes. Additional costs for the three wagons and five horses, required to provide the response to calls from the boxes, raised the total to £2,778 per annum. The cost of an individual box amounted to £8.8s.0d. each year. On 12th July 1897 the Head Constable recommended that the extension go ahead in accordance with the earlier contractual agreement and the system was certainly fully operational by April 1899.

The Head Constable outlined clearly the purpose of the facility as far as his force was concerned which included the following:

i.   To provide assistance to the public by having alarm boxes within easy reach of every part of the city by which ambulances, fire appliances and police for removing prisoners and quelling disturbances could be called,

ii. To provide communication by telephone with a central office, and

iii. To serve as a means of checking on constables in the working of their beats by means of a Reporting Key.

In Nott-Bower's view completion of the facility across the city would allow him to reduce the strength of his force by fifty men, saving £4,000. These ideas were almost identical to those claimed to be so revolutionary by Frederick J. Crawley, Sunderland's Chief Constable, when he introduced his police box system some twenty-five years later.

The National Telephone Company advertised the advantages of the Liverpool system in their sales catalogue of 1903, but the new Head Constable, Leonard Dunning, expressed some reservations even though he found it reliable. In 1906 he raised these concerns formally with the Watch Committee when the contract was due for renewal. He observed, 'As the Watch Committee is no doubt aware the present signal box is a complicated one, and the principal merit suggested for it is that the mere pulling of a lever in the box records on tape at the receiving station, the time, the place of the call, and the nature of the emergency, fire, serious fire, patrol wagon wanted for prisoner, ambulance wanted, it also provides a telephone, a visual signal by means of which the policeman can record at the receiving station the fact that he has called at the box.

It is doubtful that many of these devices are necessary, the automatic recording on the tape is seldom of any particular value, though in one or two instances it has cleared disputes as to the time of calls; the visual signal is of little value; the reporting device is of practically no value'.

Although Dunning was keen to obtain a simpler system for his force, to rely mainly on the telephone, an offer by the existing suppliers, in

Leonard Dunning, Chief Constable Liverpool City Police, 1902-1912. Credit: Merseyside Police.

THE NATIONAL TELEPHONE CO., LTD. 95

Fire, and Police Alarms—continued.

LIVERPOOL PATTERN FIRE, AND POLICE ALARM SYSTEM.

Pattern No. B123—*continued.*

The Receiving Station comprises:—Morse Telegraph Inker (with Time Stamp), and a Clock.

The Inker acts as a Receiver, the dashes sent by the Transmitter being recorded on a tape.

Fig. III.   Fig. IV.

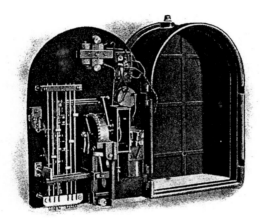
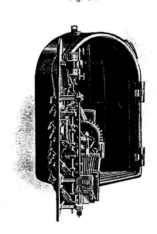

Fig. V.    Fig. VI.

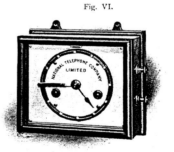

Figures I. to IV.—Fire Alarm Box.
Figure V.—Receiving Station Indicator.
Figure VI.—Clock.

Prices on application.

Publicity brochure for Liverpool Pattern System 1903.

1907, to reduce the rental from £2,100 to £1,300 for the 265 boxes then in use persuaded him to retain them. However, he did ask the National Telephone Company to quote for telephones on individual wires in street boxes with push ringing at the station and a bell that would be rung continuously at the box when the constable was required. The Head Constable felt that the number of boxes could be reduced, and by 1922, the city was served by sixty-six connected to headquarters and another 104 lines from outer division stations.

Bradford City Police was another force to use call points towards the end of the nineteenth century, although a detailed description has not been identified. In Gordon Smith's book *Bradford's Police* he describes the proposal by the new Chief Constable, Charles Paul, in 1895, to introduce a system, 'Such was Paul's relationship with the Watch Committee that by the end of the year he could report that the telegraphs in the out-district police stations had been replaced by telephones, and police call boxes were to be erected at Bradford Moor, Lidget Green, Bolton Hall, Sandy Lane, and Bolton. These call boxes were designed to be used by either police or the public in case of fire, accidents or other emergencies.' *Schemes operated by the Glasgow and Aberdeen city forces are described in the following chapter.*

The use of fire brigade facilities for police purposes was common, bearing in mind that many provincial fire brigades were under the command of the chief constable. In 1889 the Metropolitan Police agreed to communication being established between twenty-four fire alarms of the local Hornsey Fire Brigade and the police stations at Hornsey and Highgate to assist with a burglary problem in the Muswell Hill area.

The Single Wire Multiple Telephone Signal Company had, by the end of 1893, supplied about 650 of their Saunders and Brown alarm pillars to the brigade in London. The company claimed that recently patented 'loud-speaking telephones' could be fitted to the call points or wall boxes so that the fire station operator could question the caller. Although the company did suggest that their system could, if required, be switched through to the police by means of a 'simple arrangement at the fire station' the Metropolitan Police did not take to this idea.

In 1893 lightweight 'pocket telephones' were issued to some policemen in Newcastle, which, after an officer had opened the door of a fire alarm post with a personal key, could be plugged in, and communication made with the fire station. Although this link was primarily intended for reporting fires, the constable also used it to seek assistance with crimes and other matters. The fire station at Westgate adjoined the police station and the message could easily be passed on. The *Newcastle Daily Chronicle* described the telephones as, 'One of the neatest articles that has recently been added to the equipment of some Newcastle Policemen...'

At the turn of the century the National Telephone Company was a major supplier of telephone equipment including fire alarms and police signal points (as well as kiosks).

In 1909 it was suggested that their system of fire alarm pillars being operated in Bath – consisting of a transmitter, a loudspeaker receiver of the Collier Marr type and an ordinary receiver – could be used for police purposes by the Bath City Police. This system incorporated wires laid underground thus reducing the problems of damage that sometimes occurred with the overhead wires of the earlier installations. An advantage with the National Telephone Company was their ability, as the major telephone service provider at this time, to give an efficient maintenance service on their equipment. Although a facility existed on the central switchboard in Bath to extend a call to the police station it is not clear to what extent this actually occurred.

Joint fire and police facilities continued to be implemented in Britain even after dedicated police systems were becoming generally accepted as the most efficient. The Southend-on-Sea contract to install Mr Beasley's closed circuit alarms, introduced into this country in 1897, went ahead in 1924. The pillars were designed for joint use by the county borough constabulary and the fire brigade, each service having its own distinct section of the box. The fire alarms were connected to Southend and Leigh Fire Stations, whereas the police lines were linked to the police station from the separate lockable cupboard.

Police pillar, Southend-on-Sea Borough. Credit: Fred Feather.

A turret on the top of the box normally displayed a white disc that could be illuminated at night. By turning a switch at the police station the disc, visible from all directions, could be changed to red to warn the constable of a requirement to telephone the station.

These systems of fire alarms were popular and the Southend installation gave Beasley his twenty-ninth in this country. Windsor Castle's fire security relied on his alarms, and similar fire alarms were used in Manchester, Bradford, Cardiff, Bristol, Croydon and Erith. Cardiff's system of twenty-one fire alarm boxes were connected by telephone to the central fire station in 1898. Cardiff City Police, were as late as 1931, adapting fire alarms for police purposes.

Portsmouth City Police operated combined police and fire brigade pillars connected to a Beasley-Gamewell switchboard. Boxes were surmounted by a ten-inch diameter, constantly illuminated, glass globe, part blue and part orange, with a shutter that operated when the private wire circuit was activated. Interestingly, in the 1920s Portsmouth's police/firemen were not kept at the fire stations but were used to control traffic. In the event of a fire a signal was sent to the nearby pillar to alert the man on traffic control. He had to obtain a lift by tram or a passing motorcar to the fire station to board the fire engine.

Some years before the introduction of its police kiosks the city of Dundee inaugurated, in 1925, a new system of 'fire, police and accident alarms', consisting of twenty-eight red painted boxes where members of the public were required to smash the glass and turn a handle inside to speak on a telephone direct to the fire brigade headquarters. Each circuit contained no more than three boxes, therefore an abandoned call could be easily located. The posts were used for police purposes with three hundred keys issued for the police officers. Keys were also carried on the trams to enable the tramway men to make telephone calls in an emergency.

At the inauguration ceremony in Dundee the Convenor of the Police Committee, 'smashed the panel, opened the box, and called for the Fire Brigade, which was on the scene of the 'fire' in exactly 2 minutes'. No doubt they were waiting for the Convenor's test call. It is claimed that Edinburgh was the only other city in Scotland with a similar system at the time.

Fire apprentice on the Beasley-Gamewell equipment in Portsmouth. Credit: Jim Cramer.

In 1926 the Chief Constable of Derby County Borough Police decided to make far greater use of the existing twenty-four fire alarm boxes in the town for police purposes, along with a further twelve being installed. The constables were provided with keys to the boxes and could communicate with their headquarters, although there was no facility by which they could be called to the box when on patrol. A successful experiment was undertaken whereby a red light was fitted to a box and flashed to draw attention to a call. This facility was extended to the other boxes and, additionally, 'ringing in' schedules were introduced for the men on the beats. The *Derby Daily Express* described the system as 'unique this side of the Atlantic'.

Although it was not unusual for a force to use the call points of the fire brigade for police purposes, the Halifax County Borough Police seem to have been unique in their joint enterprise. From about 1906 the Town Corporation began introducing an emergency street telephone and signalling system, in the form of boxes attached to tramway standards, along the thirty-nine miles of tram routes. By 1926 there were a total of fifty-eight of these boxes in the borough used, not only for tram and electrical breakdowns, but also for fire, ambulance and police purposes

The system in Halifax was very successful and economic as it was a relatively simple matter to insert new boxes within the existing wires or, away from the tramway, wires could be run off to a box more cheaply than extending them all the way from the police headquarters. Another advantage was that the usual problems with wayleaves could be avoided and many rentals thereby saved. The switchboard at the fire station acted as the telephone exchange for the other departments using it. At about twenty elevated positions in the town, visible for miles, coloured lights were set up to draw a constable's attention to a call from the police station. It was the beat policeman's duty to test the telephone each night, any faults being reported to, and repaired by, the Corporation's engineer.

An observer of the system is quoted in the *Police Review and Parade Gossip* on its advantages, 'In former days it was not unusual to see a drunken man being dragged through the capital's streets to the Police Station, but that does not happen now, for as a Policeman now has a telephone near at hand, he telephones for the Police motor van, which is on the spot in a few minutes and the prisoner is given a ride to the Police Office.'

Whereas the first two decades of the twentieth century saw the British-based telephone companies manufacturing and supplying numerous street fire alarm systems, widely used throughout the major towns and cities, there was far less demand for dedicated police call points. Often the police facility was advertised by a supplier as an addition to a fire alarm promotion. The borough corporations obviously considered dual-purpose facilities to be much more cost effective.

In 1907 the City of London Police introduced its white cast iron pillars, bearing a red cross within a circle on the top, primarily intended for calling the electric ambulance from Bishopsgate Police Station to accidents on the busy city streets. Fifty-

City of London Police, pre-1965 post (installation date unknown). Credit: City of London Police Museum.

two of these small pillars, with telephonic communication to the police station, were installed in the Square Mile. They were replaced in 1927.

The year 1902 saw a total of 148 police forces across America using police patrol signalling systems which, ten years later, had increased to 319. Some incorporated telephones and others relied on telegraph signals; Washington, Chicago, Detroit and Boston provide examples as pioneering users of such systems. An early street telephone used by the police in St Paul, Minnesota, had two magneto generator handles, one for making routine calls to the police station switchboard and the other to indicate that a 'wagon' was required.

John Gamewell had been important in the field of fire alarm technology in the United States, and developed a police call point system there in the early 1880s. Gamewell telephones were a feature of some force facilities in this country. The company's fifteen fire alarm posts, incorporating a method whereby the firemen could plug in their portable telephones, was scrapped in Sunderland with the introduction of the police box system there.

Above: City of London Police Ambulance. Credit: City of London Police Museum. Right: City of London Police Ambulance Call Point c.1910.

There were a number of suppliers of telecommunications equipment in this country in the early years of the twentieth century. The Siemens Brothers & Co. Ltd. of Woolwich's system of police call points *(previously mentioned)* incorporated an automatic fault reporting facility. Although it is difficult to assess how successful the company was in promoting the system, it is known that Rochdale County Borough Police were operating their call points in 1905. Liverpool City Police also showed considerable interest in this facility after finding their existing facility too complex. As time went by the company, in line with others, tended towards simpler standard equipment based on a magneto telephone in a box of cast iron, and designed to meet the needs of a variety of potential purchasers.

Another notable manufacturer of fire alarms and police call devices in this country, Walters Electrical Manufacturing Company of London, established in 1880, had gained considerable experience with telegraph apparatus for the railways. Walters became major suppliers of equipment to the Post Office who often installed and maintained the company's Moore & Knight Open Circuit Fire Alarms. This system, invented in 1909 by H. Knight and refined by E. E. Moore, was first used at Sidcup and Foots Cray in 1912. Many other fire brigades followed this lead, as did the Wolverhampton County Borough Police in 1924.

The Western Electric Company was supplying small iron telephone boxes, for wall mounting or to be supported on stands, to police departments in the United States in the early years of the century. These boxes were perforated at the base in order that a passing policeman could hear a bell inside. The City of New York Police, for example, operated such a system. The company also had a base in this country and produced pillars for the British market. How well the company faired with their promotions here has not been established although, in 1924, they did unsuccessfully tender to install a system of thirty-three fire alarms and thirty-two police points at Southend-on-Sea. The company quoted a price of £3,517.12s. for a complete facility compared with £2,997 by the successful competitor, George Longfield Beasley of Merton, London.

Western Electric's telephone pillars and boxes were designed to meet the needs of any agency requiring such a facility, and often incorporated a 'plug in' removable handset which a user could carry with him to make a call to his headquarters. Apart from the pocket telephones in Newcastle *(described earlier)*, it has not been ascertained whether police used other similar systems in this country. By 1912, however, the police in Berlin had a portable plug in telephone in use presumably manufactured by a German company.

Although by the early part of the twentieth century the General Post Office were already keener to become involved in supplying and maintaining call point systems, police forces generally went their own way in selecting suppliers. The Post Office was sometimes unwilling to undertake the connections to such equipment. Some years were to elapse before the Post Office obtained the monopoly for the supply of their standard systems *(subject of a later chapter)*. It became clear by the early years of the twentieth century that the somewhat complicated telegraphic facilities supplied by many companies were not what police required for communication from the street. The telephone, coupled with suitable signalling, would fully, and more efficiently, meet their needs.

Le téléphone de police de Berlin. — 1. L'appareil portatif. — 2. L'appareil dans sa gaine. — 3. L'appareil installé sur une boîte de contact. — 4. Un poste téléphonique sur un arbre.

Police system in Berlin c.1912.
Credit: France Telecom.

Chapter 4

THE EARLY DEVELOPMENT
OF THE POLICE KIOSK (1880–c.1926)

Long before the formation of the first organised police force in 1829, or New Police as they were to become known, the watchman was one of those engaged in crime prevention in the village, town and city. Often a watch box, strategically located, provided the base from where he could carry out his duties in the neighbourhood. Many of these watch boxes, often brick built, were taken over from the parishes and remained in use by the borough police forces after their formation. In fact, it is claimed the last surviving watchman's box in Greater London, in Clapham Road, was still there in 1938.

Fixed points, namely locations where constables of the New Police would be stationed, at all or certain times of the day, were introduced as it became more difficult to fully cover the beats at regular intervals. These points gave residents confidence that they would be able to find a policeman when required in an emergency. By the end of 1870 there were, for example, a total of 207 fixed points in the Metropolitan Police area and printed notices were given to 'respectable householders' in the vicinity informing them of their location. The residents welcomed them, and gradually as time went by, shelters were erected at or near to the points, thus providing a small 'haven away from the elements' for the constable and identifying this point of contact to the public.

In the early years the fixed points in London had no facilities for communication with the police station. Although initially consideration was given to purchasing equipment from the British Telegraph Manufacturing Company, in 1871 the Post Office Telegraphs were actually requested to provide an estimate for a 'System of Wires Connecting Police Stations with Fixed Points by means of Magnetos and Bells'. The suggestion was that Sir Charles Wheatstone would supply the instruments, through the Post Office, to the Metropolitan Police. The Commissioner, Colonel Henderson, recommended renting the system from the Post Office connected to all 207 fixed points, where cast iron boxes (presumably small cupboard style fixtures) would be installed to house the equipment. By September, 1872 the full costs became apparent and it was decided not to go ahead, although the Superintendent of 'V' Division was still promoting the idea of 'telephone kiosks' some four years later.

The inefficiency of police communication from the streets was highlighted in January, 1886 when rioters caused considerable damage to property in central London as they left a meeting at Trafalgar Square. During the subsequent enquiry Lieutenant-Colonel Pearson, an Assistant Commissioner, was questioned about the facilities available to police to pass information in such circumstances. He described, in answer to a question from the committee, the system of boxes available in America. 'The mayor of Chicago gave me a description of it. It is a sort of box where a constable is always stationed, worked by electricity. By touching a certain button inside that box he can telegraph to the nearest police station, 'Assault', 'Drunken woman', 'Riot', or as the case might be; and the inspector on duty would send down the

Watchman's box in Brixton Road, London.

number of men thought necessary. You simply touch a button and either two men come to fetch away a drunken woman, or 20 men to quell a riot. They gallop down in open vans just like the fire brigade system.' He agreed that such a system was not available in London. Although improvements were made to the internal telegraph network after the riots it does not appear that any immediate action was taken to improve communication from the streets in London, apart from the apparently unrelated trials at Islington and Brixton.

The quote from a Home Office official, writing about a police box system in New York State, introduced in 1888, gives an impression of America's lead, 'As far back as 1900 I saw telephone booths as an old established part of the police arrangements of Buffalo, N.Y., and listened for a time to the constant stream of communication between the police on duty and the station.' These booths were reputedly large enough to house a prisoner pending the arrival of a wagon.

Glasgow and Liverpool were pioneering forces in the British Isles in the use of the newly invented telephone for internal communication between the headquarters and divisional stations. Perhaps their links, as major ports, with the United States,

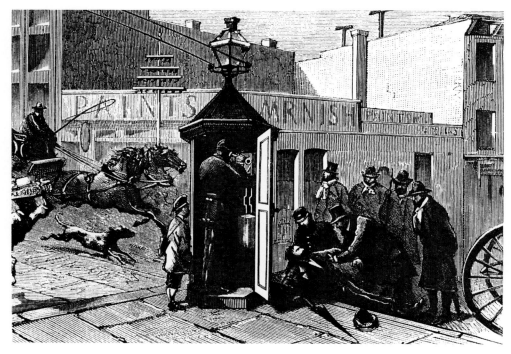

Police Box in Chicago, early 1880s. Credit: France Telecom.

where the adoption of the invention was more immediate, provided the necessary impetus. They also led the way in police communication from the streets. *(Liverpool's facility is described in the previous chapter.)*

The initiator of operational police kiosks in Great Britain, housing signalling facilities, was the forward looking Glasgow City force where, in November, 1891, the Committee of Watching and Lighting attended the central station of the fire brigade and examined an 'ornamental cast iron structure proposed to be used for the Police Signal System'. The Chief Constable, John Boyd, impressed by what he saw, obtained, from the Inspector of Fires, an assessment of the cost of erecting fourteen such structures in the city. This amounted to £17.7s.6d. for each booth with an additional £15 for the lamps and other apparatus. Painting and foundations were to cost an additional £2.10s. per box making a total outlay of approximately £500. This, of course, did not include the National Telephone Company's annual rental costs for lines and telephones of about £91 along with further maintenance charges.

The police boxes were patented by Charles Eggar and manufactured by Walter MacFarlane and Company of Glasgow. Hexagonal in shape they contained a variety of complex communication equipment. To call the attention of a policeman, a

Fig. 1. Transmetteur des signaux pour les stations d'alarme à Chicago.

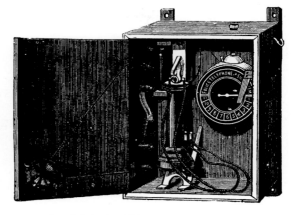

Fɪɢ. 2. Boîte de téléphone des stations d'alarme.

Call Point equipment used in Chicago, USA, in the 1880s. Credit: France Telecom.

mechanism, operated from the police station, raised a red glass globe around a gas jet on the roof of the box. Simultaneously the gas lamp ignited and its red glow could be seen for some considerable distance by constables on the adjacent beats.

Constables, holding keys to the boxes, could enter to speak on the telephone to the police office. The process of opening the door completed the telephone connection. 'Respectable citizens' also had keys, which, in common with other signalling systems, could not be released from the lock except by a policeman. The citizen established the telephone link with the station by opening the door that simultaneously ignited the gas light and raised the globe, thereby alerting the man on the beat to a possible problem. The National Telephone Company proudly advertised the Glasgow system as 'efficient, reliable, and simple' in their sales catalogue of 1903.

In 1912 plainer kiosks, built in cast iron sections and painted red, were introduced in Glasgow. These kiosks appear, in some cases, to have had electric cooking grills fitted. A standard key allowed each policeman to gain entry. The telephone facilities were exclusively for police use and not available to the public. By the end of 1931 there were ninety-one boxes in operational service, with nine more on order.

In 1898, Glasgow's neighbour, Greenock Burgh Police, introduced four kiosks where a weight, depressing a rubber gas pipe, was raised by the activation of the telephone bell. This allowed gas to flow and thereby ignite the signal lamp from a pilot jet.

Although brief references have been found indicating that call points were being used by the Aberdeen City Police at the end of the 19th century, the evidence suggests that these were, in fact, a series of sub-stations connected by telephone to the

THE NATIONAL TELEPHONE CO., LTD. 99

Fire, and Police Alarms —continued.

POLICE SIGNAL SYSTEM.

Pattern No. B125

FIG. I.   FIG. II.

A cheap, speedy, and reliable method of communicating between Police Stations in large Centres, and the constables on their beats, has long been desired by many Police Authorities. At present the system of personal messengers is slow, expensive, unreliable, and is open to many objections in other ways.

THE NATIONAL TELEPHONE COMPANY submit the system explained hereafter, as one which is efficient, reliable, and simple. Avoiding technicalities as much as possible, the following short description will show in a general way the method of operation. and how the system can be used by any intelligent citizen, without previous experience of it, also a few of the many advantages which follow its adoption.

The Signal Box is a neat ornamental cast iron structure, placed at a central point where several beats converge, and connected by a special wire with the nearest Police Office. The constables' patrol of their beats is so timed that each officer sights the box in rotation. Thus there is an arrangement by which one of the constables in the locality has always the Signal Box in view.

National Telephone Company publicity brochure advertising the Glasgow Police System, c. 1903.

police headquarters (*The Diced Cap: the story of Aberdeen City Police*, Hamish Irvine). In 1891 authority was given to construct three of these wooden buildings in various parts of the city, to be used, along with two existing police stations and a fire station, to maintain effective communication between the headquarters and the police officers in the local area. The new wooden structures were quite large, contained cells, and were supplied with hand–ambulances and fire hoses. An additional wooden sub-station was built in 1898. They remained in operation until they were replaced with larger, more secure, stone buildings in 1941.

Street alarms were not the only facility available to fire brigades. In 1901 the Hull Police Fire Brigade had six fire boxes in

Fonthill Box, Aberdeen, built in 1892.

Procession passing a Hull Police Fire Brigade Box at St Georges Road. Credit: Paul Gibson's Collection.

various parts of the city where escape ladders, pumps, buckets, turncock keys, axes, hoses and police lamps were kept for use in the event of a fire occurring in the locality. These boxes appear to have been for fire brigade purposes only with hydrants or standpipes on site to provide the water. Presumably other boroughs in the country would have had similar facilities.

The Metropolitan Police Commissioner had decided, as a result of the recommendations of the independent engineer, Campbell Swinton, and the call point trial in Brixton, that the best way forward for his force would be to erect street shelters with direct telephone links to police stations. Some suggested that it would be more appropriate to connect the existing fixed point boxes by telegraph to the divisional stations although others argued that they were unsuitable for such conversion.

Police in the capital do not seem to have progressed the new ideas for street communication until, on 13th February 1896, Henry Smith, a 79 year old man, was brutally murdered during a burglary at his home in Muswell Hill. The murder caused considerable concern in the neighbourhood with one resident, fearing for his safety, seeking direct telephone communication between his home and the local police station. The Commissioner, Sir Edward Bradford, decided that to accede to such a request could lead to an influx of similar applications, possibly overwhelming a station with direct lines. His alternative policy, to press ahead, on main thoroughfares, with the erection of police telephone boxes directly connected to the stations, would provide the reassurance sought by the public. The constable would also have his long overdue link with the police station.

On 28th March the Commissioner directed the Receiver to arrange for a box to be designed, 'Large enough to permit of the Constable standing within it with the door closed to use the Telephone instruments'. The experimental box, sited in Cricklewood, incorporated a direct telephone line to West Hampstead Police Station. It was finally used operationally for the first time in June 1897 after some unfortunate installation problems had been sorted out.

A visual device, intended to drop down thereby indicating when a call was being made from the station, had to be fitted as the original signal bell could not be heard by the constable on the fixed point some forty yards away. A much larger disc, along with a lamp, later replaced the visual indicator so it could be seen at night. The cost of the box was £20 with an estimated £13 per annum for the telephone line. Had the Metropolitan Police required wheels on the box a further charge of £4 would have been imposed.

The trial had clearly ironed out some teething problems and, in December of the following year, a Board of senior officers decreed that there should be a 'judicious extension of Telephone Boxes' in London. There seemed, however, to be no priority within the force to progress the matter and certainly no organised plans drawn up for siting boxes in the Metropolis. Although four sites were agreed immediately, not until

Metropolitan Police fixed point box converted to a telephone facility at Nunhead Park with P.C. Stephen Court outside c.1910. Credit: Metropolitan Police.

The sergeant and constables outside a pre 1929 police telephone box at Mottingham Village. Credit: Metropolitan Police.

Superintendents Davis and Mulvany visited Liverpool in 1900, to inspect the successful signalling devices there, did the project gain momentum. By 1907 some thirty telephone boxes, either purpose-built or converted fixed point boxes, were in use on the outer divisions of the force. Even a reserve box was purchased and stored for use in an emergency. In the inner area boxes were considered unnecessary, as the divisions were more compact and the stations less remote from the beats.

By 1920 the outer divisions of London were served by almost sixty wooden telephone boxes but the installation had been piecemeal and without a clearly defined objective. The concern of residents often influenced the decision to install street telephone links as, for example, occurred in Norbury in 1906 where burglary had become a particular problem. Consistently proposals for a widespread and integrated system were met with opposition. Cost was the usual obstacle although lack of use of the existing boxes featured as an excuse.

Pressure from various internal sources did lead in time to some relaxation of procedures for the man on the distant beat. There were beats where permission was given for the constable to book on and off duty from a telephone box and even take refreshments there. Police Orders and Informations relating to crimes were made available to him at the box.

Norman Mowbray, who joined the Electrical Engineers' Department in 1927 as a battery charger in the basement of New Scotland Yard, worked on the new police boxes in the 1930s and describes those they replaced, 'All Fixed Point Boxes were linked to the police station. Those I remember most are Leytonstone, Stratford, Hendon, Edgware, and Ewell by the pond. We were allowed to buy those old boxes for ten shillings and sold them to the local allotment people for about thirty shillings.

When the station rang the box, a relay dropped an indicator flag over a small hole in the top right hand window. At night an oil lamp was placed on a shelf by the window, and if the flag dropped the light from the lamp could be seen. A shelf across the back was good for a desk or your meal break. One nice thing about the old fixed point box was it had a wooden floor which made it a little more homely.'

In America the city authorities were still developing systems of policing, incorporating kiosks and associated communication features, as part of their plans. In Memphis, Tennessee, for example, an unusual scheme was introduced in 1926 where it was decided to abolish foot patrols and substitute them with motorcyclists. An inner and outer circle of 'pill boxes' were built and each fitted with a signal device, wireless receiver, automatic telephone, and a searchlight on the top. A motorcyclist was assigned to each box and five others were patrolling an area designated to the box. A crime reported to the headquarters would be sent to the appropriate box by radio or telephone. The officer on duty there would, after writing down the details and setting off a signal (the searchlight at night or an explosive audible warning during the

Norman Mowbray with his homemade Box.

daytime), leave on his motorcycle to deal with the matter. The other patrolling motorcyclists, alerted by the signal, would attend the box and, after apprising themselves of the incident, go to give assistance.

Undoubtedly other forces in the United Kingdom, in addition to those already mentioned, must have introduced police telephone kiosks on a limited scale to deal with specific problems in these early years, although research has not been successful in identifying them. Glasgow, however, appears to have been alone with anything resembling an organised policy in this respect. As far as the police were concerned it would be the 1920s that would herald the arrival of widespread and carefully planned police box systems. By this time, of course, the public telephone kiosks were increasing over the country, and having their impact on general communication.

Chapter 5

THE RISE OF INTEGRATED POLICE BOX SYSTEMS (1923–1932)

As 1923 is generally accepted as the year that saw the start of the rapid proliferation of organised police box systems in Great Britain, it seems appropriate to apply it as the date marking the end of the development stage of police call points and kiosks.

It is neither intended nor, in fact, possible to describe all police box systems introduced in many of the 250 police forces of the 1920s and early 1930s. This is just an attempt to provide a detailed description of some of these earlier facilities adopted by a cross-section of forces – mainly those with city or county borough status – where the needs often differed. Although some of the smaller borough forces installed systems soon after Sunderland most were more inclined to go ahead once the standard Post Office facilities became readily available after 1932.

There is general acceptance that integrated and organised police box systems originated with that introduced by Frederick J. Crawley, the Chief Constable of the Sunderland County Borough Police, in 1923. Although the claim seems somewhat overstated if we take account of the considerable earlier developments described in the preceding chapters. Crawley was not shy to claim credit as the 'originator' at every opportunity and in 1929 (then Chief Constable of Newcastle) even wrote to the

Frederick J. Crawley, Chief Constable Sunderland and later Newcastle. Credit: North Eastern Police History Society.

Home Secretary claiming that 'recognition was long overdue'. One official wrote of him that he was subject to 'fits of bombast and indiscretion in one of which he declined the O.B.E. for which he was recommended'. Crawley seemed to be seeking some more prestigious award but had to be content with the King's Police Medal in 1931.

Undoubtedly Crawley's enthusiasm led to widespread interest amongst chief constables and local authorities throughout the country for better communication from the streets, thereby strengthening the efficiency of their valuable manpower and improving public access to the police. More attractive to those responsible for financing the police were the claims that economies could be made by reducing the number of police stations and policemen

Crawley's system in Sunderland provides the starting point from where the new facilities throughout the country can be examined. During the ten years between the introduction of Crawley's system and the inauguration of the first standard General Post Office police pillar system, which became widely used, individual police forces erected kiosks and other call points of a variety of designs and features.

The large industrial county borough and city forces of the north of England appear to have been the most enthusiastic in initially adopting systems, although they were soon followed by others throughout the country. Prior to 1925 police in Tynemouth, Plymouth, Doncaster, Stockport, Rochdale and Wolverhampton had already followed Sunderland's lead by introducing systems.

Sunderland County Borough Police

The Sunderland police box system, introduced on 23rd April 1923, was not fully operational until July of that year. A total of twenty-two wooden kiosks, measuring approximately 4 feet by 4 feet, were supplied by a local firm, Messrs. Binns, and placed throughout this large industrial town. The green painted kiosks were positioned adjacent to the pavement; that sometimes required the removal of park railings to provide a suitable setting.

His unique police box system allowed Crawley to close down five divisional police stations, already old and long overdue for costly modernisation. In some instances the growth of the town meant that stations had become wrongly sited for the provision of an effective service to residents. The boxes, described as 'miniature police stations', provided more cheaply, with the aid of direct communication with the force headquarters, the improvements necessary. The fire alarm function was also undertaken through the new police boxes, thereby reducing the annual maintenance and rental costs substantially on the street alarm posts. The abandonment of the fire alarms did, however, receive some adverse criticism through the journal *Fire* probably emanating from those with a vested interest in maintaining such a system. The fire station and ambulance facility adjoined the police headquarters and telephone extensions allowed either to be rapidly alerted in an emergency. A fireman also drove the ambulance.

The closure of police stations, coupled with the reorganisation of the beats, allowed the Chief Constable to divert officers to operational duties and make substantial reductions in the establishment of the force. Much of the work of the police station could be carried out from the box where current written instructions, circulations relating to crime and other documents were maintained for the benefit of the man on the beat. The stool and fitted desk provided the constable with means to sit and write his reports. Advice, information and instructions could, of course, be sent from headquarters by telephone to the constable in the box.

The police operator, sitting behind his switchboard in a 'sound-proof' room at headquarters, could connect with the police boxes, departmental extensions and the Post

Sunderland County Borough Police Box, Strawberry Bank. Credit: North Eastern Police History Society.

Office exchange, thereby providing an efficient response to the demands of the public and his colleagues on the beat. In fact, the claim that, 'much will be done to counteract the popular criticism that a constable is never to be found when wanted', appears to be justified. Residents were encouraged to use the telephone, accessible from an outside cupboard; in some of the poorer areas they were gathered at a police box, with their children, to receive instructions from a constable on how to operate this unfamiliar device. In one instance a man had assumed that, after removal of the receiver from the hook of the 'candlestick' telephone, speaking directly into the mouth-piece was unnecessary. Needless to say his message was inaudible to the switchboard operator.

Switchboard duty alternated in two-hour stretches between two constables, the free officer turning out on a Triumph motorcycle combination, introduced as a feature of the box system, to calls for assistance. Private telephone subscribers were issued with instructions for calling the police as part of the scheme. A response time of five minutes was guaranteed to any part of the borough. The arrest of a violent drunk or other difficult prisoner called for the Humber motor prison van to be driven to the scene by a policeman or a fireman (designated a constable and under the command of the Chief Constable). The year 1924 saw a total of twenty-seven fire calls, 196 ambulance calls and seventy-one calls for assistance sent from the boxes.

Crawley had reckoned that on average two hours, or twenty-five percent, of an officer's patrolling value was wasted each day walking to and from his beat to report on and off duty, and to take refreshments at the police station. The new system of policing meant the elimination of this waste, there being generally no requirement to leave the beat during the whole tour of duty. Booking on and off duty over the telephone and meals taken in the police box during two quarter-hour breaks, was the alternative offered by the new system. These features of policing distinguished Crawley's police box system from those that had gone before.

The rigid laid down method for patrolling the beat was abandoned in favour of the constable's own discretion. This had the disadvantage of the sergeant not knowing the whereabouts of his staff at particular times, but the advantage of the prospective criminal not knowing them either. Supervision relied to a great extent upon the periodic telephone calls to the headquarters. The new system replaced the two split daily four-hour shifts with continuous eight-hour tours. Constables rang in to the station hourly at night and hourly and half-hourly alternately during the day.

Along with the twenty-two proper police boxes the two fire floats of the River Wear Watch (also under the Chief Constable's command) were linked to the system. This facility required gongs to be fitted to alert the boat engine-men to a telephone call. The five abandoned police stations were also designated as boxes and one pedestal type of telephone box was necessary in the town centre where lack of space prevented the construction of a kiosk.

The cost of the kiosks with their seasoned oak doors was £12.18s.6d. they were embedded into concrete with bolts by the Borough Engineer at the cost of £5 each. Additional costs included 5s.6d. for a check chain, 6s.3d. for a zinc strip plate, and £5 for electrical installations. In return for employees of the electrical company using the boxes to report breakdowns there was only a nominal charge of 5s. for power. Messrs Hiatt & Co. Ltd., of Birmingham supplied forty enamel notices for the boxes at 2s.10d. each. The early Sunderland boxes had neither visible nor audible signals to alert the officer on the beat to a call. This feature was to follow later. A woman cleaned the boxes once a week and a duster was kept handy for the policeman to use. Crawley said, 'It is always well to have a handy-man on the Force or Fire Brigade to carry out any little want, e.g. a swollen door or puttying.'

By 1st January 1925, with the police headquarters at the hub, there were a total of twenty-eight boxes connected to the central switchboard. Any box could be connected to outside calls or vice versa. The telephone connections were tested at least hourly and, if a box was found to be out of order, a constable was sent to patrol the vicinity until it had been repaired. In such circumstances it had been arranged for the officer to have access to three private telephones in the area. Unlike the fire alarms one defective line to a box did not affect others in the circuit.

Although the Home Office commented, 'I do not think we can ignore the temptation to idleness that the boxes will provide,' Crawley described his innovation as 'an unqualified success fulfilling the highest expectations'. He emphasised that his was not merely a series of street alarms, as had been the case before, but a completely new way of policing. His enthusiasm provided the impetus for other chief constables to review their policing methods and follow his lead.

By 1936 Sunderland was planning to upgrade to the Post Office's standard PA1 equipment in thirty-seven kiosks along with the introduction of two pillars.

Wolverhampton County Borough Police

The Wolverhampton County Borough Police decided on pillars as opposed to kiosks for their system and were the first force to use the Walters Moore and Knight Open Circuit equipment in this country. In 1924, on the recommendation of David Webster, the Chief Constable, the Watch Committee agreed to introduce the integrated emergency service pillars. Thirty-six standards – with communication available for fire brigade, police, and ambulance purposes – were duly positioned throughout the town. Webster subsequently wrote a letter to the company expressing his appreciation of the efficiency of the system. He claimed that about 250 calls a day were made from the pillars. An additional twenty-one call points were added to the facility in 1928.

In their sales catalogues of the early 1930s Walters Electrical Manufacturing Company describe their standard fire alarm pillar heads as being suitable to incorporate completely independent cupboards for the police and ambulance communication equipment. A normal 'break glass' fire alarm facility would trigger the fire box to open allowing the caller to use the telephone connected to the fire station. In normal circumstances only the firemen could gain access to this part of the pillar. The policeman had a key for his own side. The company claimed that combining facilities could 'lead to inefficient operation and sometimes serious misunderstanding'. Any number of boxes could be placed on to one circuit.

Mr Knight, the inventor, was engaged in installing the Wolverhampton posts and the *Birmingham Evening Dispatch* reported, 'By means of this system it will be possible, should the occasion arise, to muster the entire Police Force at a given spot within the space of about 15 minutes.' The officer on the beat's attention was drawn to a call by a 'falling disc' on the box.

Pillars were considered more durable than the wooden structures of that time and, of course, took up much less room on the streets. They did allow the closure of some police stations and a reorganisation of the system of working the beats. Constables were required to make scheduled 'rings' into the station where a large switchboard had been installed to accommodate the new facility. The total estimated cost of the system was approximately £2,000.

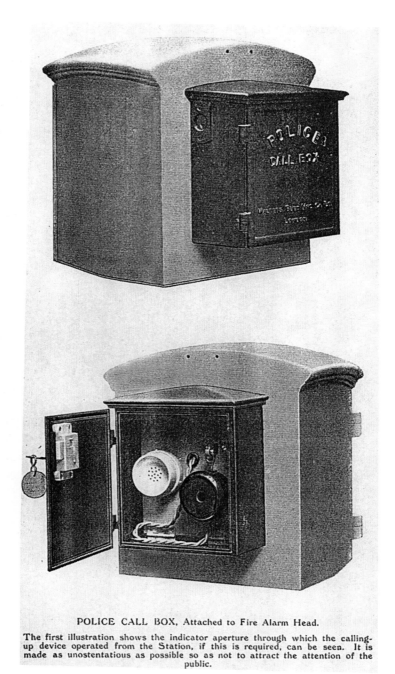

POLICE CALL BOX, Attached to Fire Alarm Head.

The first illustration shows the indicator aperture through which the calling-up device operated from the Station, if this is required, can be seen. It is made as unostentatious as possible so as not to attract the attention of the public.

The system used by the Wolverhampton County Borough Police.

A subsequent Chief Constable, E. Tilley, reported in 1933 that the system had been thoroughly reliable with no call having been lost. However, by 1936 consideration was being given to installing fifty-four of the Post Office's recently introduced standard pillars along with the same equipment in the force's one kiosk.

Tynemouth County Borough Police

The Chief Constable of Tynemouth County Borough Police, Tom Blackburn, soon followed the lead of his north-eastern neighbour Sunderland, when, on 21st February, 1925, the new call box system, which had been in use for police and public

MONDAY / THURSDAY

Beat	On duty at	1st hour	2nd hour	3rd hour	4th hour	mins. refreshments until	5th hour	6th hour	7th hour	8th hour	Off duty at
10	No. 10 Box Percy Park	1-00	2-00	3-00	4-00	5-00	5-30	6-30	7-30	8-30	Broadway & Kingsway
15		1-03	2-03	3-03	4-03	5-03	5-33	6-33	7-33	8-33	
11	Beverley Ter. & Mast Lane	1-06	2-06	3-06	4-06	5-06	5-36	6-36	7-36	8-36	Railway Station
3	Borough Rd. & Stanley St.	1-09	2-09	3-09	4-09	5-09	5-39	6-39	7-39	8-39	Railway Station
16	Waterworks	1-12	2-12	3-12	4-12	5-12	5-42	6-42	7-42	8-42	Bridge Rd. & Front St.
20	Youth Centre	1-15	2-15	3-15	4-15	5-15	5-45	6-45	7-45	8-45	Albion Rd. & Bedford St.
2	Prudhoe St. & Coach Lane	1-18	2-18	3-18	4-18	5-18	5-48	6-48	7-48	8-48	Albion Rd. & Coach Lane.
6	Albion Rd. & Military Rd.	1-21	2-21	3-21	4-21	5-21	5-51	6-51	7-51	8-51	Linskill Ter. & Wash't'n Tr
14	Delaval Av. & Heaton Ter.	1-24	2-24	3-24	4-24	5-24	5-54	6-54	7-54	8-54	Front St. & Maple Cres.
4	Howard St. & Northd. Sq.	1-27	2-27	3-27	4-27	5-27	5-57	6-57	7-57	8-57	Saville St. & Norfolk St.
7	Church St. & Tynem'th Rd	1-30	2-30	3-30	4-30	5-30	..	6-00	7-00	8-00	Church St. & Tyne St.
13	Duke of Wellington E.H.	1-33	2-33	3-33	4-33	5-33	..	6-03	7-03	8-03	Bridge Rd. & Willow Gr've
1	Alma Pl. & Preston Rd.	1-36	2-36	3-36	4-36	5-36	..	6-06	7-06	8-06	Coast Rd. Garage
8	Bird St. & Brewh'se Bank	1-39	2-39	3-39	4-39	5-39	..	6-09	7-09	8-09	Tynem'th Rd. & Tan'ts Bk
17	Hollyw'l Rd. & Langl'y Rd	1-42	2-42	3-42	4-42	5-42	..	6-12	7-12	8-12	Walls'd Rd. & Balkw'll Av.
5	Lawson St. & Coach La.	1-45	2-45	3-45	4-45	5-45	..	6-15	7-15	8-15	Wolsington Hotel
18	Moor Park Hospital	1-48	2-48	3-48	4-48	5-48	..	6-18	7-18	8-18	Lynn Rd. & Hedgel'y Rd.
9	Front St. & Bath Arcade	1-51	2-51	3-51	4-51	5-51	..	6-21	7-21	8-21	Grand Hotel
12	Cemet'ry Gates, Walt'n Av	1-54	2-54	3-54	4-54	5-54	..	6-24	7-24	8-24	Christ Church Vicarage
19	Birtley Av. & Ship'y Rd.t.	1-57	2-57	3-57	4-57	5-57	..	6-27	7-27	8-27	Entrance to Golf Course

TUESDAY / FRIDAY

Beat	On duty at	1st hour	2nd hour	3rd hour	4th hour	mins. refreshments until	5th hour	6th hour	7th hour	8th hour	Off duty at
6	6 Box, Linskill Ter.	1-00	2-00	3-00	4-00	5-00	5-30	6-30	7-30	8-30	Albion Cinema
18	Coast Rd. & Glanton Rd.	1-03	2-03	3-03	4-03	5-03	5-33	6-33	7-33	8-33	De La Rue Factr'y entr'ce
4	Camden St. & Union St.	1-06	2-06	3-06	4-06	5-06	5-36	6-36	7-36	8-36	Saville St. & Steph'son St.
12	Spread Eagle Inn	1-09	2-09	3-09	4-09	5-09	5-39	6-39	7-39	8-39	Walt'n Av. & Roseb'ry Av
13	Percy Arms, Station Rd.	1-12	2-12	3-12	4-12	5-12	5-42	6-42	7-42	8-42	Howdon Rd. & Nelson Ter.
5	Trinity St. & Coach Lane	1-15	2-15	3-15	4-15	5-15	5-45	6-45	7-45	8-45	Borough Theatre
1	Clevel'd Rd. & Clevel'd Tr.	1-18	2-18	3-18	4-18	5-18	5-48	6-48	7-48	8-48	Preston Hospital
19	Marin'rs La. & Tyn'm'th R	1-21	2-21	3-21	4-21	5-21	5-51	6-51	7-51	8-51	Knotts Flats
2	Vicar'ge St. & Hylton St.	1-24	2-24	3-24	4-24	5-24	5-54	6-54	7-54	8-54	Albion Rd. & Newc'stle St.
14	Verne Rd. & Regent Ter.	1-27	2-27	3-27	4-27	5-27	5-57	6-57	7-57	8-57	Burt Av. & The Quadrant
3	Bedford St. & Saville St.	1-30	2-30	3-30	4-30	5-30	..	6-00	7-00	8-00	Stanley St. & Rudyerd St.
20	Bedf'd St. & W. Percy St.	1-33	2-33	3-33	4-33	5-33	..	6-03	7-03	8-03	Nile St. & Russell St.
8	Electricity Works	1-36	2-36	3-36	4-36	5-36	..	6-06	7-06	8-06	Prince of Wales Tavern
11	No'th View & Eleanor St.	1-39	2-39	3-39	4-39	5-39	..	6-09	7-09	8-09	The Watch House
9	Hotspur St. & Syon St.	1-42	2-42	3-42	4-42	5-42	..	6-12	7-12	8-12	Princeway & Percy Park
17	Norham Ter. 'bus Gar'ge	1-45	2-45	3-45	4-45	5-45	..	6-15	7-15	8-15	Oswin Ter. & Balkwell Av.
16	Kingsway & Broadway	1-48	2-48	3-48	4-48	5-48	..	6-18	7-18	8-18	Plaza, South end
7	Corpor't'n Arms, Geo'ge St	1-51	2-51	3-51	4-51	5-51	..	6-21	7-21	8-21	King St. & Dockway Sq.
15		1-54	2-54	3-54	4-54	5-54	..	6-24	7-24	8-24	
16	Linden Rd. & Briarw'd Av.	1-57	2-57	3-57	4-57	5-57	..	6-27	7-27	8-27	Chirton Social Club

Extract from Tynemouth ringing in schedule.

purposes for some months, was formally introduced. The facility gave the public twenty-three points of telephone access to the police who could respond in appropriate cases in motor vehicles introduced as a feature of the system. The Chief Constable stated that the total cost of all these access points would be less than half the annual cost of one constable.

The wooden kiosks were similar in design to those installed at Sunderland but, unlike Crawley, the Chief Constable was soon to realise the need for a calling light to be fitted. Early in 1927 red lights were fitted to attract the attention of the constable on the beat to a telephone call.

It appears that by 1936 there were twenty kiosks in the town when it was decided to introduce five of the new Post Office pillars along with the installation of their equipment in the kiosks.

Devonshire County Constabulary

Captain H. R. Vyvyan, the Chief Constable of Devon, was the first to introduce into a county constabulary in the south a police box system similar to that of Sunderland, albeit restricted to the south Devon resort of Torquay. The Joint Standing Committee for the county agreed that thirteen fire alarm posts in use at the time should be removed once boxes were installed.

In November 1924 the constabulary sought an estimate for the provision of eleven four feet square, eight feet six inch high, seasoned hardwood telephone boxes incorporating a desk and drawer. Thomas Guest of Ellacombe, Torquay tendered with an estimate of £141.7s for the eleven boxes (or £12.17s per box). They were to be bolted to four inch thick concrete bases and given three coats of paint. The estimate provided for a Ruberoid matched board roof. More expensive zinc or lead roofs would have added £1.10s or £3.10s respectively to the cost of each box. Weights and axle pulleys lifted the door of the public's outside telephone cupboard. There were, of course, additional costs for telephones and their wires, although the Torquay Town Council agreed to assist financially and supply the electricity, free of charge, for the first year and possibly longer depending upon the cost. Guest's tender was considerably cheaper than those submitted by two other companies which amounted to £220 and £260.13s.

In July 1925 the Devon County Constabulary facility became operational, supported by a car kept at the headquarters to deal with calls for assistance. Prior to the inauguration the *Western Morning Express* reported that the new procedure would give the constable discretion in respect of how he patrolled his beat observing, 'This means that criminals are not in the happy position of knowing where a constable can be located at a particular time, and are unable to prearrange their nefarious designs with the knowledge that they are unlikely to be disturbed.' The *Express* suggested that there would be 'a twenty-five per cent reduction in staff and a one hundred per cent increase in efficiency'.

Although senior officers praised the system some in the lower ranks were more sceptical. A Torquay constable, writing to the *Police Review and Parade Gossip*, claimed that the boxes had reduced the number of policemen patrolling the streets leaving only fifteen to cover the whole of the town over twenty-four hours. He went on, 'The telephone boxes are situated in most isolated and quiet neighbourhoods, and the Constables on the respective beats are marching in practically a bee line, to and fro between the boxes. He is afraid to go far from that bee line because if he should happen to be two minutes late in 'ringing in' the Almighty Operator gives him a lecture…' Rather sarcastically the writer claimed, 'No wonder the Constable walks along with the sole thought of 'ringing in' and his watch in his hand…' It must be said that the writer did give an impression that he was rather bitter at not being offered an operator's post.

The Chief Constable of Devon can be congratulated, along with his colleagues in the cities of Plymouth and Exeter, as leaders in the field of police boxes in the south-west. Torquay still had eleven kiosks in 1936 when plans were in hand to introduce an additional twenty-two Post Office standard design pillars.

Exeter City Police

A. F. Nicholson, Exeter City Police Chief Constable, expressed the view, 'A Police Box System or some form of street telephone system is absolutely essential if Police Forces are not to be increased in number and by this means economies in beat working can be made which will enable men to be diverted to other duties of greater importance.'

As the head of a force in a non-industrial city in the south-west Nicholson was impressed by Crawley's police box system, seeking more information about it for the benefit of his Watch Committee, before visiting Sunderland, in September, 1924, to see it in operation. The subsequent report to the Committee later that year recommended a reorganisation of the beats and a redistribution of manpower in the force. The accepted proposal saw the force divided into eight beats for day working and fifteen during the night supported by the introduction of fourteen police boxes.

Concern that the initial price tendered for the Exeter boxes (the lowest £30 per box) was excessive led to further negotiations, particularly as those for Plymouth and Torquay had been obtained much more cheaply. Finally the City Architect accepted a quote of £270 from D. Stoneman of Whipton, Exeter, to supply and fit the fourteen boxes. There were additional charges for the electric light fittings and laying cables thereby increasing the final bill to £384. Post Office telephone and line rentals varied from between £6 and £16 for each box depending upon its distance from the headquarters. There were, of course, also annual maintenance costs.

In August 1925 the light green wooden kiosks appeared on the streets of the city and Nicholson expressed considerable pride in his new system of policing. He described a police box as a 'standing policeman', providing the public with continuous access to the station, a facility of which they took full advantage. The strength of the force stood at sixty-seven men, below the pre-war establishment and, apart from the introduction of three youths to undertake clerical posts in place of constables, no reduction of policemen could be achieved. Continuous tours of duty replaced the old 'split shifts' on the beats and one sub-station was closed. Motor transport could be called upon when the occasion demanded but none was specifically allocated to the police box system. Any part of the city could be reached within ten minutes.

The Chief Constable could find no serious disadvantage in his new system, although he did recognise that when an officer reported on duty at a box 'his condition as to sobriety and cleanliness could not be observed' by his supervisor.

Exeter City Police Box. Credit: Devon and Cornwall Constabulary.

He even accepted, 'There is ample opportunity for the 'shirker' to work his beat with the minimum of effort, and in fact neglect some parts of it altogether.' The advantages, in his view, still far outweighed the reservations.

The Chief Constable, writing about the police box system in the *Police Review and Parade Gossip*, felt that one cycle patrol in conjunction with a telephone system was the equivalent of three men on foot, and a motorcyclist was the equivalent to four and a half men on foot. He considered that, as the motorcyclist was in communication with headquarters by telephone at intervals of a few minutes, he was able to respond to an emergency call almost as quickly as being on reserve at the police station.

The first wooden kiosks had neither heating nor a method of alerting the patrolling policeman to a call from the headquarters. It is not clear whether the former was forthcoming but, over the years, the force experimented with various signalling lamps on selected boxes. A signalling system supplied by Carter & Co. (Nelson) Ltd, specifically designed for police boxes, was placed on trial at the kiosk at Exe Bridge in 1927. This facility incorporated four green bull's eye lenses set in the cast iron turret housing the lamp which, when illuminated, signified that a call was awaiting attention. The cost of the system amounted to £9.17s. Unfortunately the light did not flash, and was difficult to distinguish from other streetlights in the area. To overcome this problem, the 'interrupter' or 'scintillator', patented by Claud W. Denny of Old Bailey, London, was fitted in 1930 at a cost of £2.2s. This device caused the lamp to flash at some 120 times per minute thereby solving the problem, and appears to have also been installed in boxes in Manchester, Leeds and Newcastle.

Two additional boxes, one at Sidwell Street and the other at Heavitree, also came in for trial signalling. The former's lamp, made locally by a company named Lye,

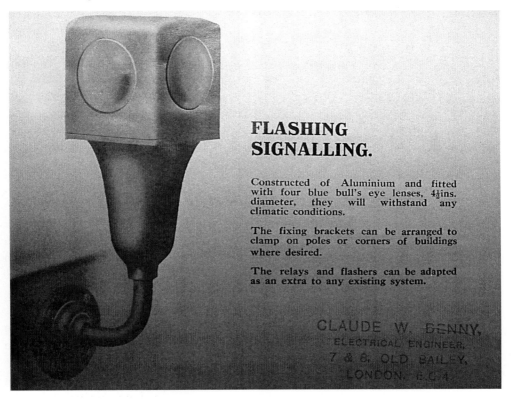

FLASHING SIGNALLING.

Constructed of Aluminium and fitted with four blue bull's eye lenses, 4½ins. diameter, they will withstand any climatic conditions.

The fixing brackets can be arranged to clamp on poles or corners of buildings where desired.

The relays and flashers can be adapted as an extra to any existing system.

CLAUDE W. DENNY,
ELECTRICAL ENGINEER,
7 & 8, OLD BAILEY,
LONDON, E.C.4.

Denny's Signalling Device.

operated through a relay supplied by Messrs. Gent & Co., of Leicester (cost £2.14s.) along with Denny's interrupter. At Heavitree the Gent and Denny equipment operated the Barcol Police Box Signal Light, supplied by Barber and Coleman of Manchester, and already in use with the Salford City police box system.

The fire brigade of Exeter, completely independent from the police force, operated a total of twenty-four Stuart and Moore open circuit pillar mounted street fire alarms in the city. By 1927 they were rapidly wearing out and becoming unreliable, having been in use for thirty-eight years. The alarms were also unsatisfactory, as line faults could not be distinguished from real alarm calls. In fact, no indication was given to a person making an alarm call that it had actually been received at the fire station. The lack of a telephone was clearly a disadvantage. Fortunately the time for replacement coincided with a need for additional street communication for the police by which time there were some fifteen police kiosks and huts connected to the headquarters.

A decision was made to abandon the fire alarm posts and to install a total of eighteen small telephone wall or pillar mounted cupboards to be used jointly, along with the existing police kiosks, for police and fire brigade purposes. A local firm, Garton and King, agreed to make the cast iron cupboards (14 inches by 9 inches by 8 inches), at a cost of twenty-five shillings each. They were duly fixed to walls, lamp standards or, at an additional one pound, the purpose-built pillars were supplied. Hiatt of Birmingham supplied the enamel nameplates and notices for fixing to the boxes. A new Post Office switchboard was installed at the police headquarters and, by the end of 1928, the new boxes were operating fully. In 1934 the total Post Office telephone rental amounted to £356.13s.6d. per annum for the kiosks and wall boxes, and by the next year a new type PA150 switchboard had been introduced.

By 1945 Exeter's wooden police boxes were deteriorating rapidly. Many were rotting and almost falling down but, due to the uncertainty about possible force mergers, a decision to replace them with a reduced number of more substantial brick structures was postponed. In fact, seven years later, reports were still being made about the state of the boxes; in one case the writer described a hole in the floor as being the work of a rat. In a drive to improve cleanliness the Chief Constable arranged for tin waste paper bins to be placed in the boxes, which were emptied on Sunday mornings by the motor patrols.

Like Crawley in Sunderland the Chief Constable of Exeter actively promoted the advantages of a police box system; consequently his advice was sought by forces, throughout the country, interested in introducing a system of their own. He willingly answered questions ranging from, whether constables were served with coffee on the beat to the problems experienced by the 'illiterate, deaf or dumb' using the facility. Nicholson's view was that the success of a system depended upon the careful study of local conditions, prior to carrying out the reorganisation necessary, to ensure that the street telephones were used to full advantage.

The Chief Constable remarked, 'I venture the opinion that the telephone box system or some system of street telephones will be looked upon in the near future as an indispensable part of the equipment of every progressive Police Force.'

Newcastle upon Tyne City Police

Frederick Crawley took up his appointment as Chief Constable of the Newcastle upon Tyne City Police on 1st July 1925, after a successful ten-year command of the Sunderland force, and ensured that this was the first major northern city to adopt his system. He soon made proposals for the reorganisation of the force. A redistribution of the strength to cater for the need to police more traffic points and to more effectively police outer areas of the city, where the population had increased substantially, required the introduction of a police box system. A trial system on the Pendower and Walker corporation housing estates was undertaken and, in January, 1926, Crawley pressed the

Watch Committee to agree to the introduction of forty-five boxes (at this time only four boxes had been installed at a cost £15 each) supported by five motorcycle combinations as response vehicles. The proposed scheme was accepted with the added advantage that the facility would be shared with the fire brigade who would dispense with their alarm posts.

Although the Home Office finally agreed to Crawley's proposals they were concerned that he had progressed the matter without their full knowledge and authority. They questioned how financial savings were to be made, and whether a proposal to transfer five police firemen, for whom Crawley was responsible, from fire duties to 'chauffeuring' the five motorcycle combinations was acceptable. Crawley appealed to the Home Office for 'a meed of real assistance' and emphasised that, 'the originating, introducing, applying and installing of the Police Box system' was pioneering work, 'fraught with customary contention and opposition…'

Newcastle City Police Box c.1928.

The Newcastle system went ahead as planned which allowed the Chief Constable to reduce the number of police stations from nine to three with the consequent savings of some twenty men. Unlike Sunderland's centralised scheme, Newcastle had separate networks of telephone boxes linked to the three divisional stations. As with other forces constables commenced and concluded duty at a box, took refreshments there and were given a considerable amount of autonomy in the working of their beats. Schedules for 'rings' to the station were changed daily to protect the constable's movements. The only time a constable needed to visit the police station was with a prisoner or to collect his pay. The sergeant would usually see one out of his six constables on and off duty but, unless a man was considered to be 'slacking', arranged 'meets' on the beat were abandoned. In the past the beats were uncovered at change of duty times whereas the new scheme meant there were in effect double the number of policemen at this time – those reporting for duty and those booking off.

Crawley opted again for four feet square wooden kiosks, as they were much warmer and cheaper than those made from other materials; they were normally placed near to street lamps. (The cost of about £13 for a wooden box compared with between £35 to £53 for an iron one.) A one bar radiator and electric light were installed; signal lamps were not as the Chief Constable felt that they would tend to keep constables in the vicinity of their boxes, awaiting a call, instead of 'exploring the extremities of their beats'. In any event Newcastle policemen rang in from a box nine times during an eight hour tour of duty, therefore the operator at the station would not have to wait too long to make contact with a beat man to deal with minor matters. The motorcycle combinations were always ready to attend the real emergencies. These response vehicles had cost in the region of £1,100, with further annual costs of some £600.

The Post Office installed their open circuit telephone system, which worked to everybody's satisfaction, although faults were not automatically registered at the switchboard, as was the case with proprietary closed circuit systems. The regular 'rings', along with use by detectives and supervisors, provided sufficient confirmation that telephones were in working order. The names, addresses and telephone numbers of at least two nearby private subscribers, who were prepared to allow the use of their telephone for police purposes should the box telephone become defective, were displayed conspicuously in each kiosk. One had to be available during the night. The station operator could, in an emergency, switch through the ordinary table type telephone, used by the public and the policeman, to a public line.

An officer now patrolled some of the larger beats, previously worked on foot, on a pedal cycle and, in appropriate places, bicycle sheds were attached to the police box. St John's Ambulance bore the cost of first aid equipment and printed force instructions were retained in the boxes. In an emergency a prisoner could be detained in a box pending the arrival of transport. An ex-constable, pensioned through ill health, visited the kiosks on a motorcycle with box sidecar, containing tools and cleaning apparatus, and carried out repairs and cleaning. During the summer months he painted them. A short broom and duster were kept at each box.

The purpose of the Newcastle system was summarised as follows

   i.   To telephone to the headquarters station on any police, ambulance, or fire brigade matter.

   ii.   For an officer to write reports.

   iii. For keeping official instructions and printed matter.

   iv.   For an officer to take refreshments.

   v.   For the detention of prisoners in certain circumstances.

   vi.   For use as a First Aid Station.

It was claimed that through the police box system the whole of the force could be mobilised within one hour.

Middlesbrough County Borough Police

On 6th December, 1926 seven police boxes, covering part of the town, were introduced by the Middlesbrough County Borough force, as a forerunner to an extension elsewhere. The initial installation resulted in Linthorpe Police Station being closed. The usual police and public telephone facilities were installed and an operator, with headphones connected to the modern headquarters' switchboard, concentrated his efforts on providing an immediate response to calls for police, fire or ambulance received from the boxes. The operator would maintain the record of the nine scheduled 'rings' made by each beat man from the boxes and, when a faulty line developed, a constable would be sent there until a repair had been effected. Two nearby private subscriber telephones, or public telephone kiosks, were available for police use in such an emergency.

The public were slow to take full advantage of the new facility, although, for humanitarian purposes (e.g. to summon a doctor), the Chief Constable, Henry Riches, did not object to callers being connected to the public network provided the constable requested threepence for the call.

Middlesbrough followed Sunderland's lead with constables parading at scheduled points daily, and working beats at their own discretion. Outside the two fifteen minute refreshment breaks constables were not permitted to spend more than two minutes in a box. The sergeant would vary visits daily to parading points as a method of supervision.

A mechanised section consisted in 1929 of two motorcars, two motorcycle combinations and one patrol van. These vehicles were used to answer calls from the boxes. By 1936 there were twenty-six kiosk type police boxes in the area.

Burnley County Borough Police

In mid–1925 the Burnley Watch Committee in Lancashire proposed that the police in the borough should adopt a police box system similar to that in Sunderland. This received Home Office approval in October that year. Seventeen kiosk type boxes, fitted with telephone, electric lighting, a stove, stool and desk, were to cost an estimated £19.10s.9d. each. The St John's Ambulance Association provided first aid equipment. Additionally a further seven small telephone call boxes, costing £5 each, were to form part of the system. The annual charges for the system were estimated at £300.

The introduction of the facility resulted in the closure of three police stations and a reduction in the police strength from 134 to 126 men. The estimated savings were in the region of £2,000 per year.

The scheme came into operation in January 1927 and soon the Burnley Magistrates were commending a Mr Brooks for utilising a police box in the early hours of the morning to inform police about a shopbreaking; his information resulted in an arrest. Later that year the Chief Constable, W. Fairclough, submitted his report on the system that indicated that it had been a complete success with no false alarms reported. He said, 'There is also a sense of security both to the public and to the Police, as a telephone call will bring assistance by motor vehicles to any part of the borough within five minutes whether it be for police, ambulance or fire brigade.'

Under the scheme police constables became responsible for districts rather than the usual beats giving them a greater sense of responsibility.

Manchester City Police

In July 1927 the new Chief Constable of the Manchester City force, John Maxwell, with the members of his Watch Committee, visited Sunderland and Gateshead where they examined their police box systems. The increase in the number of housing estates in Manchester, along with the requirement for more police officers to be employed on traffic control duties, meant that it had become impossible to efficiently cover all the existing beats. Areas which had previously been agricultural were built upon and police stations were often, therefore, wrongly located. Additionally the stations were old and in need of renewal or substantial repair. A police box system, coupled with a reorganisation of the beats, provided a welcome way to overcome many of these difficulties and generally improve efficiency.

A trial on a limited scale soon went ahead and, towards the end of 1928, the Chief Constable's proposal for an extension requiring the amalgamation of two existing divisions received the Watch Committee's approval. The new scheme relied upon efficient transport, consequently two motor ambulances, which could be converted into patrol vans, and four motorcycle combinations formed a fleet. Pedal cycles were to be introduced for patrol purposes on a number of the beats that, together with the

Manchester City Police Box. Credit: Greater Manchester Police.

extensive box system and motor transport, enabled the Chief Constable to enlarge beats considerably.

On 1st April 1929 the police box system formally came into operation on the new 'C' Division. Each beat had its own 'beat box' and, additionally, 'emergency boxes' were installed. All had telephone communication with the divisional headquarters at Mill Street. The division was divided into six sections with three beats forming each section and one of the boxes designated the 'section box'.

As with earlier systems, policing methods were changed making the boxes the 'centre' for patrolling the beats rather than the sub-divisional stations. The constable was permitted to work his beat in a manner 'he considers best in the interests of the Force'. The usual selection of printed instructions and forms were kept in the boxes.

The boxes were of wood framing, about five feet square, on a concrete base. A washbasin was provided. The closure of five sub-divisional stations released three sergeants and twelve constables for patrol duty. Two constables operated the switchboard at the divisional headquarters with its forty-six telephone lines.

In 1936 'B' and 'C' Divisions in Manchester had a total of eighty-six kiosk type police boxes and the Post Office's PA150 switchboard had been introduced.

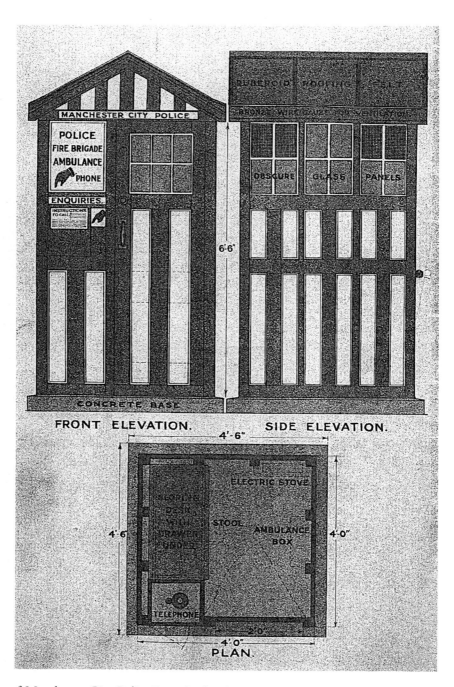

Plan of Manchester City Police Box. Credit: Greater Manchester Police.

Sheffield City Police

By November, 1926 the Chief Constable of the Sheffield City Police, Percy Sillitoe, was seriously considering a police box system and reorganisation of the methods of patrolling the beats. The introduction of the system some time later allowed the force to operate with four divisions instead of six, and to close eight small police stations. A proposed augmentation of staff was reduced substantially.

By 1929 one division was completely equipped with forty-six kiosks, located about one half mile apart; sites selected provided the maximum visibility. (The plan was to eventually introduce 150 boxes throughout the whole of the city.) A washbasin and water supply was available in the five feet square boxes that were built of wood framing, with cement inserts. The cost of each box, excluding the erection and lighting charges, was in the region of £13. The telephone system was rented from the Post Office. The first aid kit could be accessed from outside by the public breaking a glass panel and removing a key to open a cupboard. A penalty of £20 was threatened for improper use.

A patrol wagon was attached to each division to provide the response to calls from the police boxes over the direct telephone lines to the divisional stations. An indication on the station switchboard as to whether the call came from the public or a policeman ensured that the female operator responded correctly. The Sheffield boxes supported a blue signal lamp on the roof so the divisional headquarters could keep in touch with the man on the beat.

Sheffield operated the system in a similar fashion to that in other forces in that constables no longer visited the station to report on and off duty or to take refreshments. The 'conference box' (one on each beat) contained the papers, files and printed information required by the man on the beat.

R. Howard, a retired Sheffield police officer, describes in the *Journal of the Police History Society* (1999 issue) the removal of the boxes that had survived the Second World War, 'Having been a cabinet maker as a boy I was one of the individuals partially responsible for their removal and dissection. The wooden structures consisted of 2 inch x 2 inch framing clad with ¾ inch tongued and grooved timbering with an

Sheffield City Police Box 1927.

outer framework suggesting a mock Tudor half timbering. The panels were filled with wire mesh and coated with cement. Structurally most of them would have survived another 30 years service upon their retirement.'

Metropolitan Police

The most extensive police box scheme was that commenced by the Metropolitan Police at the end of the 1920s. As a trial the force erected two police boxes on the Becontree Estate at Dagenham in Essex in 1928 after tenders had been obtained from six companies. Messrs. Groves and Sons and Messrs. Thomas and Edge submitted the lowest estimates for the wooden boxes, the former with a stone roof, priced at £38.10s., the latter supporting a wooden pyramid roof, at £39. An additional £1.8s. provided for a ventilating panel showing the word 'P O L I C E' and there were, of course, other costs for lighting and telephone connections.

Fully fledged experiments on the Richmond ('V' Division) and Wood Green ('Y' Division) sub-divisions were approved early in 1928, and included changes in the methods of policing. This involved the erection of police telephone kiosks at a junction

Metropolitan Police kiosk and van, 1930s. Credit: Metropolitan Police.

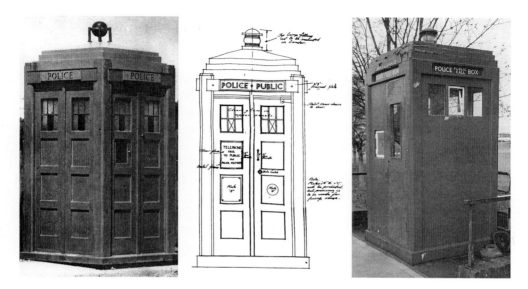

Left: An early wooden Metropolitan Police Box used with the new scheme c.1930. Credit: Metropolitan Police. Middle: Extract from a design drawing for the standard Metropolitan Police concrete kiosk. Credit: Metropolitan Police. Right: A later much plainer Metropolitan Police Kiosk at Hendon Training School.

of two or three beats, and the provision of two cars and one light van for responding to calls made from them. Variations in the supervisory duties of inspectors were also introduced. The Metropolitan Police did not, however, adopt the Sunderland system whereby constables reported for duty from their beats, but continued to hold formal parades at the police station where officers could be properly briefed and inspected by the sergeant. Crawley was scathing about this practice reporting that, 'The Metro police still follow the Victorian method of marching and file like geese from the stations whilst the extremities of the beats are left to marauders'.

All constables were, as systems became operational, issued with beat books giving *Instructions on the Working of Beats and Patrols* on the sub-division. These books indicated how a beat was to be worked and provided a schedule of 'ringing in' times (varied day by day). Retired P.C. Bill Beer remembers the 'ringing in' procedure when he was serving at Walthamstow on 'J' Division in the late 1930s, 'There were four schedules A, B, C, and D and according to each, you patrolled the beat clock or anti-clockwise, ringing in at one or other box adjoining your beat or patrol. On the outer beats you always took (½ hour) refreshments at a box. Often you were expected to book off from one or other box. They were not comfortable to take refreshments in and often, halfway through, one would be called away to deal with an accident or some other incident in the vicinity.'

On 2nd December 1929 at 6 a.m. twenty-two boxes went into operational use in the Richmond, Barnes and Kew areas of the capital. The boxes, supplied by Groves, were of the now familiar design, credited to the Architect and Surveyor to the Metropolitan Police, Gilbert MacKenzie Trench, but built of wood and not concrete. They were coloured blue and supported a red signal lamp. A candlestick type telephone, connected to Richmond police station, could be used by police officers from inside the box, and by the public opening a cupboard outside. The van, introduced in connection with the new scheme, carried equipment to deal with accidents, breakdowns and other occurrences.

The cost of the initial forty-three boxes for Richmond and Wood Green was made up as follows –

G. Groves & Sons – for boxes	£1,615.18s.6d.
Patent Victoria Stone Co–concrete roof	£189.0s.0d.
Dales – name plates	£60.4s.0d.
Wood Green UDC – altering railings	£3.10s.3d.
R. Couper & Sons – altering cupboards	£9.11s.10d.
Engineering Branch Services	£545.19s.8d.
Total	**£2,424.4s.3d.**
Telephone Rentals	£741.16s.6d.

In January 1930 Wood Green's twenty-one police boxes were operational and clearly such installations were to be a permanent feature of policing London in the future. In addition to the extension of the new style boxes across the force area, about fifty of the old pattern fixed point boxes were upgraded with modern facilities. This included fitting a telephone cupboard for public use and affixing a notice indicating that it was a police box. The cost of conversion amounted to about £8 per box.

In 1930 companies were again given the opportunity to submit tenders for the supply of boxes for the completion of 'V' Division. The following quotes were subsequently received for each box providing there was a minimum order of fifty –

Wood with Concrete Roof (as existing experimental boxes)	
Groves and Son	£38.10s.
Cast Iron, George Wright Ltd.	£56
Crittal Manufacturing Co.	£59.15s.
H. Hope (not less than 100)	£55
Concrete, Norwest Construction Co. Ltd.	£47.10s.
Somerville and Co. Ltd.	£42

Concrete provided a more durable material and, in due course, an order for twenty-five such boxes, at £43 each, was placed with Somervilles. This enabled 'V' Division to be completed by April 1931.

The Home Office gave approval for the system to press on with all speed, and by 1934, the outer divisions of 'K' and 'R' had been completed, along with a large proportion of 'Z', 'P', 'W' and 'Y'. Minor modifications to the design had included a change to the pierced 'POLICE' panel, that could not be easily seen and resulted in a draught inside the box. The red globe type signal lamp was later changed to a sixty watt white light, designed by an engineer at New Scotland Yard, throwing beams around the box similar to that on a lighthouse. An explanatory notice was affixed to the box to encourage public use. The St John's Ambulance badge displayed outside would signify the availability of a first aid box.

Norman Mowbray, who was involved in wiring up the concrete police boxes in the 1930s, says that their electric heaters were inadequate and officers constantly complained of the cold. He recalls comments like, 'How would they [the originators of the system] like to sit here on a cold winter's night to have their meal break with spiders dropping on your sandwiches?' Heaters were changed from 80 to 250 watts in 1933.

It seems that initially the police box circuits terminated on a separate private wire switchboard at the police station although the Post Office did approve, in 'occasional' circumstances, connection with an exchange line. Although, George Abbiss, a Chief Constable of the Metropolitan Police with responsibility for the system, was opposed to using the Post Office's standard street equipment their new Ericsson switchboards and associated equipment, suitably modified, were agreed in 1932 for 'Z' Division (Croydon, Wallington, Norbury and Streatham) and areas that followed.

Unlike the provinces the Metropolitan Police did not attempt to close any police stations as a direct result of introducing police boxes, although it does appear that Knights Hill Police Station on 'Z' Division did not survive. Similarly there was no intended reduction in policemen, although some adjustment of supervisory ranks was necessary.

Lord Trenchard, Commissioner of Police, 1931-1935.

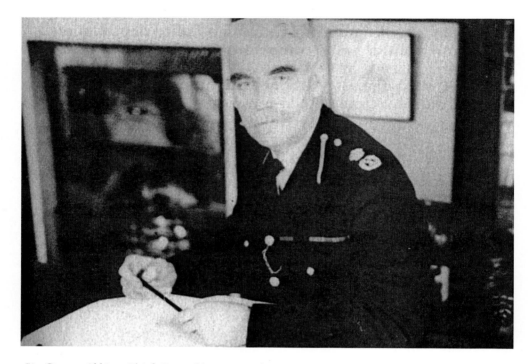

Sir George Abbiss, Chief Constable, Metropolitan Police, appointed Assistant Commissioner in 1936. Credit: Metropolitan Police.

In 1932 George Abbiss expressed concern to the Post Office about delays on the 'Z' Division project, nevertheless, by the end of 1933, throughout the force area, 168 new boxes were in use along with fifty-one converted fixed-point boxes. Delay in progress prompted a letter from the Commissioner, Lord Trenchard, to Colonel Sir Donald Banks of the Post Office, in October, 1935, seeking his assistance, 'I leave this office on 11th November, and, knowing you are a live wire I thought I would ask you, if there is any delay due to your people, if you would kindly ginger things up. I dare say some of the delay is all our fault, but really do not care in the slightest whose fault it is as long as we get on with the job. Yours sincerely, Trenchard.'

How successful Trenchard's letter was in speeding up the process is not certain, although the number of boxes in operation had risen from 335, at the end of 1934, to 581 at the close of 1936; by this time a decision had been made to construct pillars in the more congested parts of the capital *(see the following chapter)*. The Commissioner's Annual Reports of the 1930s expressed some concern about the reluctance of the public to resort to the police boxes to make contact with the police. The private telephone was already having its impact in reducing the necessity for such a system as far as the public were concerned.

An innovation that would have an increasing impact on the need for police boxes was the formation, in June 1934, of the Information Room at New Scotland Yard to where the public were soon to be encouraged, using the number WHItehall 1212, to report emergencies, particularly relating to crime. In 1937 this access to the police was improved even further by the introduction of the '999' system that, in due course, went nationwide.

In 1938 police boxes in the Metropolitan area totalled 662 along with fifty-eight posts. Between January and April that year there were 4,000 calls from them made by the public. The estimated installation costs at that time had amounted to £37,650 and the annual maintenance costs, including telephone, electrical charges, cleaning and repair, amounted to £34,150.

Leeds City Police

The Watch Committee for the Leeds City Police decided in 1925 that some of the divisional police stations should be closed, during certain hours of the day, and substituted by a police box system modelled on that in Sunderland. Opinion was divided as to whether this was a sensible course of action, even though it was proposed to install a telephone outside those of the twenty-two stations which were subject to closure. The Leeds Police Fire Brigade, also under the Chief Constable's command, were operating sixty-seven alarm points in the city at this time, but presumably, they were not suitable for police purposes.

Although the reorganisation would have resulted in a saving of constables required for clerical duties, no actual reduction in strength could be achieved due to the need to divert officers to the rising demands of traffic duty and the increasing urbanisation of the city.

The proposal did not proceed until some four years later, when the decision to install boxes on one division as an experiment was made by the Chief Constable, R. L. Matthews. The six existing police stations, in the area selected, were to

Leeds City Police Box with powerful light.

be reduced to one located at Chapeltown. Thirty-six boxes, connected by direct telephone line to this main station, were due to be fully operational by January 1931.

The blue and white painted, four feet square, wooden boxes, built by Messrs. Pullan of Beeston, Leeds, were sunk into concrete bases. The windows were of neutral tinted glass, allowing the constable to see out, but preventing the public from seeing in. The telephone and first aid box were accessible from the outside by the public. A lift-up lid on the desk inside varied from the usual drawer, and an electric radiator provided for the constable's warmth. Those on point duty outside, during cold weather, were supplied with hot coffee conveyed to them by a motorcyclist.

The outstanding feature of the Leeds box was the square red Selenium signal lamp on its flat roof. This light flashed about 120 times per minute when it was necessary to call for the attention of the constable, and could be seen one and a half miles away. In fact, this was the largest signal lamp to have been introduced at that time by any force.

Kingston-upon-Hull City Police

The police in Kingston-upon-Hull were operating with fifteen kiosks in the city in 1930 when the Watch Committee agreed to the introduction of an additional thirty-three boxes (eleven in east Hull, twelve in west Hull and ten in the centre) at a cost of £2,061. The city had increased substantially in area and population at the

Hull City Police Box at James Reckitt Avenue. Credit: Hull City Archives.

Hull City Police Box, Southcoates Lane. Credit: Paul Gibson's Collection.

time. Eleven sixteen–year–old youths were to be employed as switchboard attendants for the scheme, costing £572, and were earmarked to become constables on reaching the age of twenty. Two police stations were to be closed.

In May 1931, the new system had been introduced successfully into east Hull, followed in April, 1932 by west Hull, and finally the central area. The Chief Constable, Thomas Howden, felt that, with a police box system in place, the beats could be enlarged thus avoiding any increase in the existing strength of 472 men. Had it not been for the scheme an additional sixteen extra constables would have been required at an annual cost in excess of £3,300. It seems that eventually Hull had a total of sixty police boxes installed.

Leicestershire County Constabulary

Previously boxes had been restricted to the towns and cities when Captain C. E. Lynch-Blosse, the Chief Constable of Leicestershire, decided for the first time to inaugurate a police box system in a rural area of a county force. Lutterworth Section, one of the most rural in the county, was, prior to 1931, policed by two sergeants and eight constables and was selected as the first area to have police boxes installed. The boxes were placed in the villages of Arnesby, North Kilworth and Ullesthorpe operated from Lutterworth Sectional Station. The area comprised of 47,000 acres with a population of 10,000.

Police personnel were reduced to one sergeant and six constables. The whole area was 'mechanised' with a motorcar and motorcycle combinations supplied for their use. The officers saved by the system were absorbed into motor patrol duties. In the villages where the boxes were introduced village constables were withdrawn and the area covered by the officer on the beat.

Unlike the system introduced into cities and boroughs the Leicestershire system had no direct telephone link with the police station, but was connected to the public exchange. When a constable on the beat was required the sergeant would telephone the exchange operator who would ring the box. If an officer was not present a disc indicator would drop down indicating to the constable

A surviving Leicestershire Constabulary Police Box at Newtown Linford, 2004.

making his next visit that he was required. He would telephone the exchange and ascertain from where the call had emanated.

First thing in the morning a constable remained in the box for thirty to forty-five minutes for the benefit of local inhabitants. This, in effect, made the box a miniature police station. When the constable was not there the telephone instrument was kept locked up so that the public could not make unauthorised calls. To gain access to the telephone to make a call a resident had to break the glass of the case containing the key.

The boxes, designed by William Keay, were about five feet square and lined with wood. There was no heating in the box and no illumination due to the remote situation. In 1934 the Chief Constable claimed that people had stopped complaining about the removal of the village constables. He further reported that his constables 'no longer vegetate in a village, but keep much more alive and alert through having more to do over a wider area'.

Some Other Early Systems Around the United Kingdom

The Chief Constable of Doncaster County Borough Police, William Adams, decided, after visiting Sunderland in 1924, to adopt a similar scheme by substituting the existing twenty-two fire alarms with twenty-nine police boxes. That year the Chief

Plymouth City Police Box in Eggbuckland, 1954. Credit: Plymouth City Museums and Art Gallery Collection.

Constable of the Plymouth Borough (subsequently City) Police, Herbert Saunders, also sought tenders for police boxes of a design like those used in Sunderland. In due course Messrs. Pearn Brothers made these at a cost of about £20 per box and by January 1925 a small system of wooden boxes was operating in the borough.

In September 1926, the Watch Committee for Aberdeen visited Newcastle to examine the police box system as they were considering introducing a similar scheme for the Aberdeen City Police. The existing system had been operating for over thirty years and an extension was needed due to the growth of the city. By 1929 there were eleven boxes in the city, when authority was given to introduce a further twenty-seven. Selected boxes were designated 'beat boxes' where constables reported on and off duty.

Glasgow's proposed reorganisation in 1926 to police a larger city area, with new housing schemes and increased traffic, would place more reliance on boxes and vehicles. By extending the beats it was felt that a saving of £50,172 could be made in the first year and £53,827 the following year.

Also that year the Liverpool City Police, another force with a long history of street call points, were considering an outlay £25,000 on a combined police

Aberdeen City Police Box. Credit: Grampian Police.

telephone box and fire alarm system consisting of two hundred installations.

Approval was given in October 1926 for thirteen reinforced concrete boxes to be installed in the Gravesend Borough Police area at the cost of £550. The scheme was claimed by the Chief Constable, A. G. Martin, to be the first in the south of England. The boxes were to have room for fire, ambulance and first aid equipment. The constables would parade for duty at the boxes and the public would have access to their facilities.

The Chief Constable of Dewsbury County Borough Police, S. Barraclough, decided to go ahead with a scheme similar to that in Exeter, and, in due course twelve boxes were positioned throughout the town. Newport County Borough Police in Monmouthshire had been considering the installation of a Beasley system but, at £4,000,

Aberdeen City Police concrete Box at Rubislaw. Credit: Grampian Police.

was too expensive. Again a system similar to Exeter's was more affordable for the borough.

By 1927 the Chief Constable of Shrewsbury Borough Police, Frank Davies, who had become dissatisfied with the unreliable fire alarm system operating in the town, was anxious to introduce police boxes. He saw the value of constables being contactable whilst patrolling their beats. The Great Grimsby County Borough Police had introduced a system of boxes in April where constables proceeded straight to their beats and rang in to headquarters hourly.

On the south coast Brighton County Borough Police decided, in 1927, to introduce twenty-five wooden police boxes. They were weatherproofed and bolted to concrete bases in such a manner that they could be easily removed. Motor transport was a feature of the scheme with the estimate for the boxes and a light car amounting to £1,025.

Brighton Borough Police Box.
Credit: Sussex Police.

Brighton's neighbour, Eastbourne County Borough Police, were faced with opposition when a proposal to close a police station, and introduce a number of 'lodges' for policing the town, was put forward. The idea was to use gas lighting in the boxes, as it was cheaper than electricity, and would allow constables to heat their food on a gas ring.

By 1929 police box schemes had clearly taken off as the new method of policing throughout the country. Stockport County Borough Police had eighteen in use, Cambridge City thirteen, Worcester City twelve and Reading County Borough had purchased five boxes at a cost of £17 each. Salford City Police were using boxes large enough to house a bicycle and in Wakefield the City Police introduced a system of nineteen boxes along with motorcycle combinations as response vehicles. In Hastings the borough engineer had drawn up his sketch plans for a wooden box. In November of that year the Leicester City Police received approval to install thirty-nine boxes, over a period of three years, at a cost of £1,850; this would be fully compensated for by the closure of

Stockport Borough Police Box.
Credit: Greater Manchester Police.

Cambridge City Police Box. Credit:
Cambridgeshire Constabulary.

Leicester City Police Box (Post War Picture).
Credit: Leicestershire Constabulary.

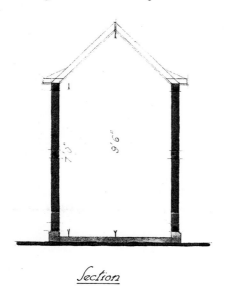

Part of a sketch plan for Hastings Police Box,
1929. Credit: East Sussex Record Office.

Salford City Wooden Police Box. Credit:
Greater Manchester Police Museum.

four police stations. Nottingham City Police, which had for many years used fire alarm telephones for police purposes, had a number of timber built boxes (7 feet 6 inches by 5 feet 8 inches) operating with blue signal lights.

The Mayor undertook the formal inauguration of the seven Winchester City Police boxes in July 1929, when he sent a test message from the Airlie Road box requesting an ambulance. The Chief Constable, W. G. Stratton, was keen that the public made full use of the telephone facility to call the police, fire brigade and ambulance. When required an ambulance was used as a police van. The boxes were built of concrete and painted dark blue. One police station closed as a result of the introduction of the scheme.

In 1930 Bradford City Police formally introduced a scheme with in excess of one hundred boxes, a large proportion having facilities to prepare meals and some had hand washbasins fitted (*Bradford's Police* Gordon Smith). Earlier boxes had had red lights fitted. In 1934 the force used wireless for the first time on one of their motorcycle combinations.

After the Chief Constable of Wigan County Borough Police, Thomas Pey, expressed concern, in 1930, about the public's reluctance to use the telephone in the town's police boxes, the local director of education was asked to arrange for children to be given appropriate instruction in the schools.

Bradford City Police Box. Credit: West Yorkshire Police.

Swansea Police Box. Credit: By permission of South Wales Police Museum.

In 1931 Southend-on-Sea County Borough Police opened its new box system. Crawley, then Chief Constable of Newcastle, was present to receive congratulations from the Mayor and Chairman of the Watch Committee as the originator of the scheme. H. Maurice Kerslake, the Chief Constable, stated in his address that 'imitation was the sincerest form of flattery'.

As early as 1925 the Chief Constable of Great Yarmouth County Borough Police had examined the Exeter system, although it does not appear that the order for three kiosks, at £20 each, was made by the force until 1931. By 1933 there were five boxes on the outskirts of the Ipswich County Borough Police area. The Chief Constable, keen to establish a suitable refreshment system for his constables, had written to the Exeter force enquiring whether coffee was supplied to the men on the beats. The reply was that they took their own Thermos flasks, and left them in the boxes when they commenced duty.

In June 1934, the Norwich City Police scheme, that had been installed some years earlier, was completed with the last link in the chain of boxes surrounding the city. The boxes had been installed on all the new housing estates. The Chief Constable, J. H. Dain, present at the demonstration of the system, said that the police were anxious to prove they were servants of the public and do everything possible to prevent crime. The boxes would assist them to achieve this.

Police boxes appeared in a number of other forces by the 1930s, including the county borough forces of Huddersfield and Swansea, and York City.

Rather than introduce expensive police box systems some chief constables were, by 1926, negotiating with the Post Office to allow the use of ordinary public telephone kiosks, without charge, to call for police assistance in an emergency. No '999' system was available at this time. The new Chief Constable of the Reigate Borough Police, W. Beacher, even arranged in 1931 for his constables to attend nominated public telephone kiosks on their beats at scheduled times during the tour of duty. When a beat man was required by the officer at the police station the kiosk telephone would be 'rung' at the appropriate time. However, by 1936, even Reigate considered that twenty-two pillars in the town would be more effective, although it is not clear when this installation went ahead.

The development of the police box during the ten years from 1923 had seen additional facilities often included, depending upon local policing methods; signal lights, cooking rings, washbasins and cycle storage all became features where they were considered desirable for efficiency. It is claimed that by 1931 a total of eighty towns had adopted a system, along the lines of that in Sunderland *(Appendix A lists the early systems that have been identified)*. This indicates how rapidly police boxes became an important feature of policing in Britain. Police forces in other countries, including Australia, Denmark, Holland and Sweden, were also showing an interest. Soon systems, particularly incorporating pillars, would become even more popular with the General Post Office's adoption of Ericsson equipment as their standard, thereby over-shadowing other brands, although kiosk design continued to vary from force to force.

Police Box at Almondbury, Huddersfield. Credit: West Yorkshire Police.

Chapter 6

STANDARDISATION OF SYSTEMS
(1932–c.1960)

By the end of the 1920s it was becoming clear that a considerable market existed throughout this country and abroad for police box systems. The diversity of proprietary equipment presented difficulties for the General Post Office, who were normally responsible for the direct telephone line installations and their maintenance. This diversity meant that it was unable to hold stocks of standard spares and delay in rectifying faults therefore occurred. The switchboards at police stations varied from one force to another, and the Post Office were generally opposed to allowing connections, through proprietary equipment, between the direct lines and the public network on the grounds that there could be abuse. An extensive network of underground cables had been laid by the Post Office since 1920 making connections easier to install and maintain. Standardisation of pillars and telephone equipment would undoubtedly result in economies for both the Post Office and the customer.

During the 1920s Captain Peter Doig M.C., who had been with the Royal Corps of Signals, saw the potential for standard emergency service street call point equipment and associated switchboards. This resulted in his design and subsequent patent (applied for in March, 1929 and accepted in June, 1930) of 'A Telephone and Signal System for Fire alarm, Police and Ambulance calls and the like'. Doig's patent included a facility whereby the opening and closing of a door on a pillar activated switches allowing immediate communication with the central equipment. A visible signal and a facility to identify faults were built in.

Obviously Doig needed a company to develop, manufacture and market his system and, in July 1929, he reached agreement with Ericsson Telephones Ltd. to do this, also negotiating the royalties he would receive. Over the period that followed Doig and the company refined the original design, and further patents were applied for. Ericsson demonstrated an early model of the system to the police authorities at the police headquarters in Glasgow in 1930. By the following year a triangular prism head had been designed for the pillar; this would become an outwardly recognisable feature throughout the streets of the Britain for many years.

The borough forces of Renfrew and Johnstone were absorbed into the Renfrewshire Constabulary in 1930 and soon the Chief Constable, John Robertson, placed orders for Ericsson installations in the two towns. The benefits of the new system were demonstrated through the experience gained in these towns and soon other forces became interested. In 1933 tests were carried out on the system by engineers from the Post Office Engineering Research Station.

The PA1 Police Pillar and Kiosk Equipment

The success of the Ericsson equipment soon encouraged the General Post Office to adopt it as their standard design for street police call points. They were to be identified by the code PA1, and either presented as a pillar or adapted for fitting in a new or existing police kiosk. The police authority concerned generally ordered kiosks independently with the design catering for the subsequent fitting of PA1 equipment.

Gaining purchasers for the new system depended to a degree upon successfully promoting its benefits to chief constables and other interested parties. Prospective purchasers would be loath to change unless there were obvious financial gains or advantages in respect of efficiency. The Post Office, of course, did have the advantage of a monopoly in respect of telephone lines, which obviously guided prospective buyers towards their equipment.

In June 1932 L. Simon, Director of Telegraphs and Telephones for the General Post Office, addressed the Chief Constables' Association with a lecture, entitled *The Possibilities of the Telegraph, Telephone and Teleprinter Service as Affecting the Police and Fire Brigades*, in which the advantages of the new Post Office call point system were emphasised. This presentation followed the publication, the previous month, of a descriptive sales brochure for the apparatus. These brochures, later entitled *Post Office Standard Police Kiosk or Pillar Telephone System*, were revised over the years, and widely circulated to interested parties throughout the country. The brochures impressed on readers how many forces had already successfully installed the facility.

The PA1 street facility incorporated separate telephones for police and public use. Within the pillar a transmitter, activated by the process of pulling and holding open a cupboard door, merely required the private caller to direct his speech towards the grille when communicating with the police station. The reply from the police came over the loud-speaking device located within the same grille. The absence of a telephone handset made the process simple for the caller and it was felt at the time that the public would, therefore, be more willing to use it. It also reduced the possibility of malicious damage to the equipment. Identical equipment could be installed in police kiosks. A continuously illuminated lamp, activated by use of the

SHOWING THE SIMPLICITY OF PUBLIC COMMUNICATION WITH THE POLICE STATION.
To call—pull and hold open the Door. The door is self-closing; being controlled by a robust spring and oil buffer mechanism. There are no cords to be cut or to perish and the line wires are led in by underground cables.

GPO publicity showing public use of PA1 Pillar.

street telephone, indicated to the policeman on his beat that a public call was in progress and the person making it may need assistance.

The constable used a separate telephone handset either located in an adjacent locked cupboard on a pillar or, in the case of a kiosk, accessible from the inside. An indicator on the central switchboard would show whether it was a police or public

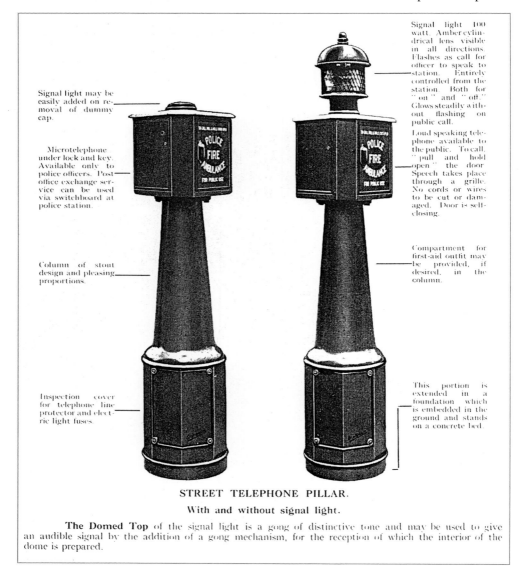

Signal light may be easily added on removal of dummy cap.

Microtelephone under lock and key. Available only to police officers. Post office exchange service can be used via switchboard at police station.

Column of stout design and pleasing proportions.

Inspection cover for telephone line protector and electric light fuses.

Signal light 100 watt. Amber cylindrical lens visible in all directions. Flashes as call for officer to speak to station. Entirely controlled from the station. Both for "on" and "off." Glows steadily without flashing on public call.

Loud speaking telephone available to the public. To call, "pull and hold open" the door Speech takes place through a grille. No cords or wires to be cut or damaged. Door is self-closing.

Compartment for first-aid outfit may be provided, if desired, in the column.

This portion is extended in a foundation which is embedded in the ground and stands on a concrete bed.

STREET TELEPHONE PILLAR.

With and without signal light.

The Domed Top of the signal light is a gong of distinctive tone and may be used to give an audible signal by the addition of a gong mechanism, for the reception of which the interior of the dome is prepared.

GPO PA1 Pillar publicity.

call. The flashing light or an audible alarm, activated from the switchboard, indicated that the officer on the beat was required to receive a call. These lights with a lattice effect surrounding the glass and a gong atop, were either fitted to the top of the kiosk or pillar, or in some other prominent clearly visible position nearby. A 'pull-down' writing shelf on the pillar allowed the policeman to make his notes whilst on the telephone.

The street points worked on a principle of party lines and, in 1932, the Post Office's PA101 switchboard, designed by Ericsson specifically to meet the needs of the new police system, became widely installed in forces outside London. This switchboard incorporated three panels, the centre for normal Private Branch Exchange (PBX) circuits and the outer two for the call point terminations. The City of London Police required a special switchboard, designed in 1933, to allow for twenty of its eighty existing call points to be easily set up for broadcast calls. The PA101 required a modification to meet the needs of the Metropolitan Police, who did not operate PA1 standard pillars; similarly their kiosks incorporated only one telephone handset apparatus for both police and public use.

The PA101 was soon found not to suit the requirements of many other police forces and, in 1934, after investigation by the Post Office, a newly designed switchboard, the PA150, became the standard for police purposes. Initially direct dialling from extensions to the public exchanges could be arranged if specifically sought by the purchaser, but the high demand for through dialling, made the facility a necessary built-in feature of such switchboards by 1937. This modified switchboard became known as the PA150 TD and was then adopted as the British Post Office standard for police. A PA150, built to meet the specific needs of the Metropolitan Police, was coded PA150 MP and another variation, coded PA190, catered for the large number of street points and extensions required by the Bradford and Glasgow City Forces.

The widespread use of the PA1 Pillar

Numerous forces throughout the United Kingdom rapidly took up the PA1 street pillars and kiosk equipment, either as a replacement or upgrade for an existing system or a completely new facility. The ready availability encouraged many of the smaller borough forces and county constabularies, previously without police boxes, to adopt a system. Where a constabulary adopted a scheme it was normally concentrated in the town divisions and not throughout the county. In many places, the PA1 pillars were more suitable and economic than kiosks, occupying little space in the busy streets of a town and costing less to install and maintain. From a distance, it was claimed, they could even be mistaken for a policeman.

Ericsson were convinced their system was imperative for effective policing and stated in their *Bulletin* in 1933, 'The speedy collection and distribution of information

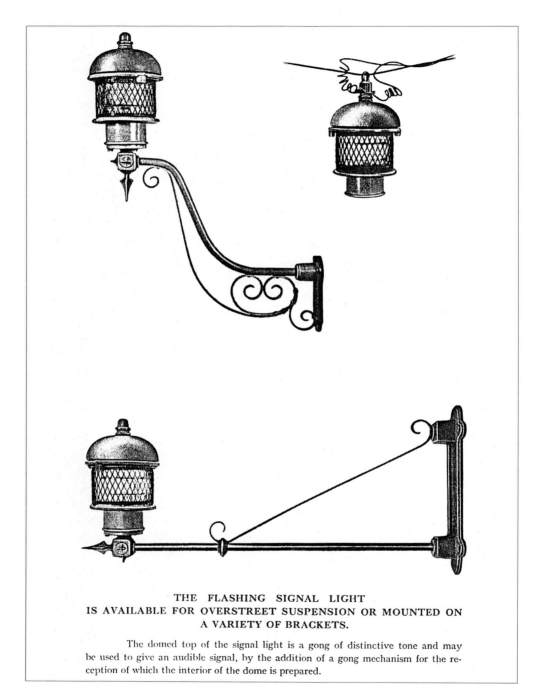

**THE FLASHING SIGNAL LIGHT
IS AVAILABLE FOR OVERSTREET SUSPENSION OR MOUNTED ON
A VARIETY OF BRACKETS.**

The domed top of the signal light is a gong of distinctive tone and may
be used to give an audible signal, by the addition of a gong mechanism for the reception of which the interior of the dome is prepared.

GPO Police Telephone and Signal System publicity. 1932 light fitting.

is the basis of all police attack on crime and the day is not far distant when it will be regarded as essential that a police communication point should exist at practically every street corner.' The company were able to demonstrate the system at their works at Beeston, near Nottingham.

The Edinburgh City Police became the first force to introduce the PA1 pillars, and similar communication equipment in their beautifully designed police boxes, through the Post Office. The feasibility study into a box system had been commenced in 1928 (before the standard Post Office equipment had been designed) by the Chief Constable, Roderick Ross. Ross decided that a major reorganisation should be undertaken involving the reduction of divisions from five to four and the closing of many police stations. Staff reductions of three inspectors, ten sergeants, and eighteen constables were also possible.

The formal inauguration of the new Edinburgh system took place in May 1933, although clearly it had been in operation for some time prior to that date. The system was acclaimed as the most modern and advanced in the United Kingdom, and the Lord Provost praised the police for their progressiveness. The system provided 154 telephone call points throughout the city giving the public an efficient method of obtaining police assistance. On the switchboard a white light indicated that a fault had occurred, a green one that a call was being made by a policeman and a red one that a member of the public was calling. The signal lights on the Edinburgh boxes and pillars were coloured red. The existing street fire alarms were in due course dispensed with. Crawley, Newcastle's Chief Constable, was present at the inauguration receiving praise for his original idea from Ross. Crawley in turn described his counterpart as 'the most able and striking personality in British policing'.

In the course of installing the 141 police boxes and thirteen pillars over five hundred miles of underground and overhead circuits had to be provided; clearly a major undertaking. The cost of £15,260 for the system was, however, well and truly compensated for by the economies made by reducing police stations and staff.

The other main Scottish city, Glasgow, became an early user of the new system. In November 1932, the innovative Chief Constable, Percy Sillitoe, who had expressed concern about the effectiveness of his new command, had started a reorganisation of the Glasgow force. Sillitoe had arrived from Sheffield City Police the previous year where he had been instrumental in introducing an extensive police box system.

Sillitoe decided that a new police box scheme would not only aid him in his resolve to improve efficiency but would also give the public a much needed means of making contact with the police. Concrete kiosks, similar in design to those introduced by the Metropolitan Police, would replace the existing metal ones, and incorporate the Post Office's PA1 equipment. This would provide separate telephone facilities for the police and public. The implementation was to be spread over five years.

The Glasgow system seemed to mirror that of the Metropolitan Police (with the exception of the telephone facilities) and the published objectives were identical –

For the Police –

i.   to communicate information to, or obtain advice, information or assistance from the Station, and for dissemination of urgent information and messages requiring immediate action;

ii. to report to the station at certain or prescribed intervals;

iii. as a place in which Sergeants and Constables will take their refreshments during prescribed periods;

iv. to prepare, when necessary, reports on occurrences; and

v.   for emergency signals from the Station.

For the Public –

i.   to obtain immediate communication with, and, if necessary, prompt assistance from the police;

ii. to make enquiry or obtain advice on any matter within the range of police duty; and

iii. to obtain assistance in cases of urgency for humanitarian or other legitimate purposes.

Many other forces in Scotland were using, or seriously considering installing, a system during the 1930s. Giffnock, near Glasgow, had a facility by 1935, as had Motherwell in Lanarkshire. In 1937 the Chief Constable of the Greenock Burgh Police agreed that, where there were no Post Office public telephones in the area, urgent calls for medical assistance could be sent to the police station from a police box or pillar for passing on to the doctor. He felt that this concession would be good for police/public relations.

In England the county of Lancashire had a substantial number of city, borough and county borough police forces within its boundary, most of which enthusiastically adopted the new Post Office system. It appears that Blackburn County Borough Police were the first to adopt such an installation along with the Post Office's PA101 switchboard at the headquarters. From 6th June 1933 the first group of beats

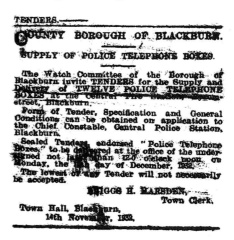

Tender publicity for Blackburn boxes.

were being worked by the new system, including two of the five new rural beats. As boxes and pillars were completed, the facility gradually extended to cover all beats in the force area.

Rural out-stations were closed (apart from one at Copy Nook which was utilised as a police box), and bicycles were kept in the appropriate box for patrolling these areas. All boxes were supplied with police publications, daily crime information sheets and lists of lock-up property and key holders. Even an ink well and pen were on the inventory. A Police Constable Rigbye took up his appointment as box cleaner, with an additional responsibility to deal with any defects and keep stores stocked up. The Blackburn system was reported as a success by the Chief Constable in his annual report the following year, apart from some apprehension on the part of the public to make full use of it.

St Helens County Borough Police followed Blackburn that year and soon neighbouring forces were sending representatives to look at existing facilities with many subsequently adopting their own. Presumably one police authority in the area would not wish to be over-shadowed by a neighbour with the up to date technology. Rochdale and Preston County Boroughs had systems by 1935, soon followed by Bolton. Oldham, however, continued to use the old street fire alarm system, introduced in the 1890s.

The Lancashire County operated a system of police pillars in Seaforth in 1933 and, by 1938, it seems the areas of Denton and Stretford also had systems in operation. The Mayor in the Accrington Borough Police area inaugurated, in late 1937, a system consisting of seventeen pillars connected to the headquarters' switchboard. The value was soon demonstrated when a constable telephoned from a pillar to his headquarters the details of a stolen car he had seen pass. To his delight a motor patrol was alerted and, after a chase, arrested the culprits.

Prior to the introduction, in September 1933, of the Post Office's street pillar telephones in a part of the Birmingham City Police area, the police had used a number of fire telephones. The new pillars incorporated a blue signal light on the top controlled from Kenyon Street Police Station, which gave out a steady light when a member of the public was using the telephone device. In 1937 the force were still only operating eleven pillars connected to the central switchboard, even though the system had proved very satisfactory. An extension to other divisions was under consideration with plans to increase the number to twenty.

Borough and city forces of the home counties also realised the value of the system when, in 1933, the Rochester City Police decided, after consultation with the Corporation, to introduce a scheme consisting of twenty-five pillars and two kiosks in the city and the adjoining town of Strood. A number of the other borough forces in Kent adopted systems that passed to the constabulary with the 1943 amalgamations. A retired Kent police officer, S. Spice, recollects eight boxes and six pillars in the town of

The Kent Police Museum has replicated a shield above the light found on some pillars during wartime.

Tunbridge Wells. During the War it seems that the pillars in Maidstone were fitted with a shield above the light to deflect the beam downwards, so it could not be picked up by enemy aircraft (presumably other forces used similar devices).

The Reading County Borough Police, Berkshire, another early user of the new Post Office facility, was running a kiosk and pillar system of thirty-two call points by March 1934. In line with other forces a call from the public for assistance would cause a red light to appear on the switchboard indicating the number of the box and a green light would denote that a constable was calling from the police side of the box. The *Police Review's* reporter claimed, 'The policeman's instrument is so amplified that he can whisper into [the telephone] the description of a suspect who may be standing only a few yards away, although the officer at the other end can receive the message clearly and give any directions necessary.' The Chief

A concrete box in Ramsgate, Kent. Signal light PA1 style. Credit: Kent Police Museum.

Constable, T. A. Burrows, claimed the system put his force ahead of any town in the south of England. The new loud-speaker method had obviated the previous problems whereby the public had generally been shy to use an ordinary telephone handset. The annual cost amounted to an increase of only about £20 over the previous system.

Bedford Borough Police had introduced a system, and the St Albans City Police, Hertfordshire, put into operation a total of twenty-four kiosks and pillars in September 1935. In St Albans amber seems to have superseded red as the colour for a signal lamp. The usual first aid kits were available for use, particularly with road accidents. The St Albans facility featured extensively in Post Office publicity material. At the inauguration of the Luton Borough scheme in 1937 the Chief Constable, George Edward Scott, addressed members of the public who had gathered in front of a new box for a demonstration.

Chesterfield Borough Police introduced a system of kiosks and pillars in February 1934 (this appears to have been an improvement on an earlier facility), handling 445 calls that year from the public. The system allowed a reorganisation of the force including the closure of two police stations. The nearby forces of Derby County Borough and Newark Borough went ahead with Post Office systems.

The Lincoln City Police introduced a PA1 system in 1934 and, in October of that year, the Chief Constable sought advice from the Post Office about whether improper use of a pillar by the public amounted to an offence. Theft of electricity, provided the telephone had been used, seemed to be the only possible grounds for a prosecution. The county force had introduced boxes at Cleethorpes by the end of the decade.

By 1935 the Chief Constable of Dorset County Constabulary was planning the introduction of sixteen concrete kiosks and fourteen pillars in the town of Poole. The kiosks were to cost in the region of £47 with the system based on the PA1 equipment. Later records indicate that there were only eight pillars and one box in the town. The neighbouring Hampshire town of Bournemouth (later to become a County Borough force in 1948) also adopted a system during the 1930s. Pending completion of the police box system in Southampton County Borough the Chief Constable, Frederick Tarry, in 1942, directed his officers to use air raid wardens' posts for routine and emergency communication.

The inauguration of the new Gateshead County Borough Police Ericsson system in August 1935, provided the benefits of PA1 equipment in sixteen kiosks throughout the town linked to the headquarters. The Chief Constable, Mr Ogle, even hinted that,

The Chief Constable addressing the public at the inauguration of the Luton Borough Police Scheme 1937. Credit: The men who wore the straw helmets by Thomas Madigan.

Woman Police Officer in Portsmouth using a PA1 Pillar. Credit: Jim Cramer.

in the future, telephone messages from headquarters might be automatically recorded in the box in the absence of a constable. Other county borough forces in the north-east were upgrading their out-dated street communications, including the South Shields police where twenty-five kiosks and eighteen pillars were planned for Post Office equipment in 1936.

The 1930s saw the majority of the borough and county borough forces in Yorkshire introduce the Post Office system. By 1935 the West Riding Constabulary had set up a sophisticated network of telephone communication, from its headquarters in Wakefield, with lines also connected to the borough and city forces in the county. The Chief Constable, Lieut-Col. Brook boasted, 'Hence you could have any police box in Bradford getting in touch almost immediately with any police box in any part of the county.'

In 1935 the Brighton County Borough Police upgraded their police box system with the installation of the new equipment. Other towns in the region followed Folkestone Borough and Hastings and St Leonard's-on-Sea County Borough.

The Newport County Borough Police in Monmouthshire set up a PA1 pillar and kiosk system in April, 1935, where, in one instance, the calling lamp hung over the centre of a wide junction making it visible to the maximum number of men on the beat.

Although Cheshire County Constabulary planned to have an extensive system in the divisions of Altrincham (three kiosks/ twenty-three pillars), Crewe (twenty-seven pillars), Hoole (twenty-one pillars) and Sale (one kiosk/ twelve pillars), it does not appear that this contract went ahead. The neighbouring Staffordshire County Constabulary, however, did begin to erect a system just prior to the war; it is claimed that by 1948 there were a total of 291 pillars in the force area.

The Post Office generally advised police authorities to paint their pillars red (presumably this colour was cheaper and easier for the Post Office to maintain as it matched their kiosks and post boxes). Although many forces used red, others did not, leading a Post Office official to comment, 'The result is that throughout the country we are treated to a variety of patterns, some pillars are red, others blue, some blue and white and others green and white. This catalogue does not complete the tale.' The Post

Surviving Police Box in Newport, Gwent with painted 'Dr Who' scarf, 2004.

Opening of the system in Leamington Spa, 1941. Credit: Terry Gardner.

Office maintained the view that a generally recognisable colour for both boxes and pillars would provide a more efficient public service.

By mid–1935 a total of thirty-two forces had introduced the new Post Office system with another nine planned for that year. The number of such installations exceeded seventy by 1939 (*Appendix A*). Just prior to the war Macclesfield Borough Police introduced a system followed, during the war, by installations in the Wigan County Borough Police and Leamington Spa Borough Police areas. It also seems that, during this period, the county borough forces of Warrington, Wallasey and Birkenhead had systems installed.

Interestingly, Ericsson had estimated in 1937 that there was an overall market for ten thousand of their call points. It is doubtful that they actually achieved the apparently worldwide assessment.

Soon the 1943 and 1947 amalgamations in England and Wales would result in the majority of the remaining borough and smaller city forces being absorbed into the county constabularies, leaving the county boroughs and larger cities with independent forces. Similar amalgamations took place in Scotland. Existing police box schemes from the absorbed forces would, as a consequence, become the operational responsibility of the county chief constable; for example, the Lancashire Constabulary had reputedly, in 1950, a total of 193 boxes, many presumably inherited from the old borough forces of Lancaster City, Bacup, Ashton-under-Lyne and Accrington.

The Development of the PA2 and PA3 Pillars

Installation of the PA1 equipment continued outside London until the early 1950s by which time some forces were looking for a more suitable system to meet the needs of the time. Although the Metropolitan Police decided early on to use the Ericsson PA101 switchboard, suitably modified, and subsequently the PA150 MP, George Abbiss, the Chief Constable with a responsibility for communications, had objected to introducing the PA1 street equipment generally accepted elsewhere. The Post Office were not too pleased with his decision, but Abbiss always maintained that its loudspeaker telephone device would actually discourage the public from making routine calls to the police station. In any event the Metropolitan Police were keen to experiment further to ensure that any system they used met the needs of the force.

The Metropolitan Police pressed ahead with their familiar concrete boxes until the mid-1930s by which time the installation programme was reaching the more congested inner divisions around the West End. In these areas large enough sites could not generally be found on which to install kiosks. An alternative, other than the unsuitable PA1, had to be found which suited the needs of the force. This led Gilbert MacKenzie Trench, the Architect and Surveyor of the Metropolitan Police, to design the long rectangular shaped pillar that became the substitute for the kiosk in central London. This post incorporated similar communication facilities to the existing concrete kiosk and contained sufficient space to store a first aid kit, fire extinguisher and, when necessary, the policeman's cape. The flap of the cupboard below the telephone cabinet could be utilised as a writing shelf.

The initial requirement for twenty-five pillars led to tenders being received from three companies. The lowest quote from Messrs. Carron & Co. amounted to £471.7s.6d. (including £102 for the patterns). Additional orders over and above the first batch would cost £15 each.

The first of these new call points was commissioned at Piccadilly Circus on 14th December 1937. During the early part of 1938 the completion of 'A', 'C', 'D' and 'E' Divisions saw the whole force served by either kiosks or posts and, prior to the outbreak of War, the number of boxes and posts amounted to 730 overall.

By 1953 the Metropolitan Police were using a total of 685 kiosks (a few were communication points set up in existing police buildings) and 73 posts when the Home Office, with the support of many chief constables, raised the concerns with the

Metropolitan Police Post from 1937. Credit: Metropolitan Police.

Post Office about the efficiency of the PA1 street call points used outside the capital. The loudspeaker on the public side of the PA1 attracted unwanted interest and this, it was claimed, deterred persons from making use of the facility. By then people were more comfortable using a standard style telephone than a loudspeaker. In addition police authorities wanted more storage for police equipment than was available in the PA1 pillar, that only had room for a first aid kit. The posts, being used successfully by the Metropolitan Police for many years, provided these requirements.

Resulting from the representations the Post Office developed a new system, designated the PA450, incorporating new PA2 pillars identical, except in some detail, to those used by the Metropolitan Police. This new system had direct lines to a standard PMBX switchboard, in effect, a standard installation with additional special equipment for the extensions to the call points. The advantages over the existing system were the use of a normal handset by the public, a simplified circuit dispensing with the microphone and loudspeaker, making it less liable to interference, and standard components allowing easier maintenance. The proposed system, having been approved by the Home Office with the backing of the chief constables, was supplied by the Post Office for new installations. (Plans, drawn in 1954, for a more modern style of post do not seem to have proceeded beyond the design stage.)

The new PA2 pillar was larger than the PA1, and in due course constructed of cast iron. As the Metropolitan Police had already developed the pattern it was immediately available for casting; it would weigh in the region of seven hundredweight. The cupboard at the bottom contained the signalling unit. The switches controlling the internal lighting, and for testing the signal lamps, were in the compartment below the telephone cupboard. The top compartment contained the telephone and internal lamp for illuminating the perspex police signs around the top of the post and on the compartment door. This door was fitted with a door closing spring to prevent it being inadvertently left open. The yale key was carried by all constables to open the middle and lower compartments.

The same PA2 call point telephone equipment could be adapted for use in a police kiosk. It was designed for termination on lamp calling switchboards although, for smaller installations, could also be used on indicator calling equipment.

On 22nd July 1954 the first of the new schemes started in the Cardiff City Police area where a standard PBX switchboard was used. Initially this system supported a total of nineteen PA2 pillars, with a further twenty-six planned for early the following year and a final total of ninety by 1956. Certainly the system gave better performance in respect of line utilisation and transmission.

By the end of 1954 the Post Office planned installation programme was well under way with the following systems anticipated by forces throughout the United Kingdom within the forthcoming two years.

Replacing a PA1 with a new PA3 in Norwich c.1963. Credit: Norfolk Constabulary.

Force	Street Call Points
Lincolnshire County Constabulary	29 posts/8 kiosks (Scunthorpe)
	13 posts/4 kiosks (Grantham)
Newcastle City Police	54 posts
Bristol City Police	69 posts (?)
Bristol Port Authority	25 posts
Cambridge City Police	29 posts/6 kiosks
Leicester City Police	25 posts/44 kiosks
Leeds City Police	33 posts
Salford City Police	34 posts
Rotherham County Borough Police	40 posts (?)
West Suffolk Constabulary	3 posts (Bury St Edmunds)
Dudley County Borough Police	17 posts/10 kiosks
Bournemouth County Borough Police	5 posts/35 kiosks
Peterborough Combined Police	40 posts
Great Grimsby County Borough Police	41 posts
Coventry City Police	79 posts/58 kiosks
Cardiff City Police	90 posts
Dumbartonshire County Constabulary	9 posts/1 kiosk (Alexandria)
Angus County Constabulary	7 posts (Arbroath)
	3 posts (Forfar)

Provincial force installations continued with obsolete pillars gradually being replaced by the new structures. The PA2 pillars were supplied and maintained by the Post Office on a rental basis, whereas only the telephone, line and signalling equipment were provided and maintained for a kiosk on this basis. The kiosk structure remained the responsibility of the local police authority. The signalling lantern used on the PA1 equipment continued to be used on the provincial force kiosks. The installation of an audible alarm, in addition to a visual signal, on either the pillars or the kiosks was possible.

The weight of the PA2 had made it difficult to install. This resulted in an identical design, using much thinner metal, being developed. The new post, designated the PA3, became standard issue from 1958. Weighing only two hundredweight, with no need to sink the base far below ground, it could be secured by bolts to a concrete base.

By the 1950s a number of county forces had, or were, introducing schemes in their main town divisions. Durham County Constabulary, for example, had systems in Darlington and West Hartlepool, and Northumberland in Whitley Bay and Wallsend. By 1952 Bridlington in the East Riding had a scheme, and the end of the 1950s saw Hertfordshire introduce pillars in Watford. The Fife Constabulary operated a system in

Dunfermline and West Suffolk at Bury St Edmunds. The contrast in the size of schemes was considerable with the small town of Tredegar in Monmouthshire Constabulary and Bury in Lancashire, seemingly operating with one pillar in the town centre.

The amalgamations of the mid and late 1960s would encourage the chief constables of the newly constituted forces to review any acquired police box and pillar systems to establish whether they could be reduced in size, or abandoned altogether. By this time the majority of the seventy-five or so county borough and city forces, along with the larger Scottish burgh forces, that remained prior to amalgamation, from Inverness in the far north to Plymouth in the south-west had adopted a General Post Office scheme of one form or another. In contrast no such consistency existed in the county constabularies. Whereas a few had introduced systems in divisional towns, or inherited them from previous amalgamations, others, like the constabularies of the north of Wales and Northern Ireland, appear to have had no boxes or pillars at all. Very few forces, however, were using pillars other than those offered by the Post Office.

A selection of surviving police posts. Left: Metropolitan Police post at Northwood police station. Middle: City of London Police post on Aldersgate Street, London. Right: City of London Police post at the Avoncroft Museum of Buildings. Note minor differences between Met post and others.

Chapter 7

POLICE KIOSK AND CALL POINT,
EQUIPMENT AND USE (1923–c.1960)

The introduction of the integrated police box systems from 1923 led to a proliferation of different kiosks, pillars and wall units and associated equipment, much of which has been described in the preceding chapters. Although generally pillars were becoming a standard design from the 1930s, kiosks, provided on behalf of the local police authorities by many companies, varied considerably throughout the country. Even within the same force area boxes occasionally differed depending upon the function they were to perform. Using examples and personal recollections an attempt has been made to identify the variations in facilities and their use throughout the British Isles.

Prior to the 1930s a large proportion of the kiosk type of police box introduced by forces throughout the country were built of timber and of a design not unlike a sentry

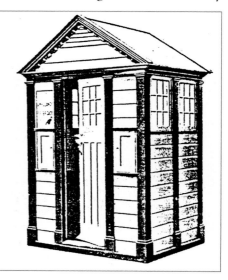

B309 Police Boxes

Police Boxes and call stations for ambulance, fire brigade or road service associations, differ in detail, and requirements change from time to time. For this reason no stock is held, but any quantity can be prepared at short notice to a specific design.

Large numbers of these types of buildings have been supplied by us in different parts of the country, and the standard of construction is fully approved. The boxes are made in sections to facilitate assembly, and removal if necessary.

We shall be glad to submit designs with full specifications upon application.

Extract taken from a 1938 Boulton and Paul catalogue.

box. The designers and builders were generally local to the area concerned although it is clear that their ideas followed those that had gone before. A force considering introduction of a system would obviously consult another with one already in operation. The Chief Constable of Exeter, for example, received enquiries from no less than thirty forces seeking advice and guidance, and in 1929, as the Metropolitan Police were about to introduce a system, George Abbiss and Gilbert MacKenzie Trench, visited Salford, Manchester, Sheffield, Nottingham and Birmingham, to gain information about the arrangements in these forces.

Timber, although it did not stand up to the elements as well as other materials, provided a cheaper form of construction thus accounting for its early popularity. Reportedly the wooden structures were warmer than those of other material. One company, Boulton & Paul of Norwich, advertised prominently wooden police kiosks in its sales catalogues of the 1920s along with potting houses, sheds and bus shelters.

As wooden boxes deteriorated concrete became a popular replacement material, although wood certainly remained prominent up to the War and, in some forces, continued until the system was eventually abandoned. Retired Police Sergeant Keith Rigg remembers the green wooden boxes in Eastbourne in the 1960s, particularly one located on a dangerous bend as a steep hill entered the town; ideally positioned to be struck by an out of control vehicle!

As noted before the Gravesend Borough Police was considering reinforced concrete boxes in 1926 and the Winchester City Police was another early pioneer of concrete. The familiar Metropolitan police box, introduced in 1930, however, really aroused interest in concrete, and similar designs subsequently spread to some other forces. Apart from a few minor variations the concrete kiosk in London remained un-changed over the years, although a much later design did have a plainer appearance. In some forces, such as Sheffield City Police, cement coated wire mesh panels were used on a wood framed construction.

A number of companies, in different parts of the country, were offering concrete police boxes. The Concrete Unit Co. Ltd. of Trafford Park, Manchester offered their 'Stonehenge' cast stone products and advertised the boxes as proving, 'far superior to the usual wooden structure as they are practically everlasting and need no painting or other preservation'. Tarmac Ltd., of Wolverhampton also produced a box for the local force.

The South Shields County Borough Police introduced, in August 1930, unusually shaped concrete boxes, designed by the Borough Engineer, J. P. Watson. The boxes were of seven sides bolted together with galvanised iron brackets. There were three leaded light side windows and a Columbian pine panelled door. The pointed roof gave the appearance of an Arabian tent (it has been suggested that this design resulted from the town having a substantial Arab population) and supported a red electric

South Shields police box at Tyne Dock. Credit: Photographic Archive, Beamish Museum.

signal light operated from the central police station. The Croft Granite, Brick and Concrete Co. Ltd., of Croft near Leicester, supplied these boxes, which were painted red and black.

In January 1934, the Plymouth Watch Committee gave approval for the erection of a new concrete box on trial in the city. In due course the precast concrete boxes, supplied by F. J. Moore Ltd, of Pomphlett, near Plymouth, replaced the sixteen wooden kiosks in use at the time. The company claimed their boxes were 'made in sections which interlock, and can therefore be easily erected by any local builder'. It seems that Norwest Construction also provided a concrete box in the city costing £85. The Salford City Police also replaced, as an experiment, one of its wooden boxes with a concrete version that year, and Stoke-on-Trent City Police introduced its first three kiosks, built of

Stoke on Trent police box. Credit: Alf Tunstall.

concrete by a local company, Ball and Robinson, at a cost of £75 each. These boxes contained, in addition to the usual equipment, pyrene and foam fire extinguishers.

Cast iron in the construction of police boxes goes back to the ornamental hexagonal shaped kiosks used by the Glasgow City Police at the end of the nineteenth century. By the early 1930s the manufacturer of those structures, Walter MacFarlane & Co., of Saracen Foundry, Possilpark, Glasgow, was offering newly designed cast iron kiosks and pillars for sale. The kiosks were of two types, of almost identical size (about 4 feet 6 inches wide by 6 feet 4 inches long by 8 feet 6 inches high), costing £47.13s and £41.15s. respectively, with additional installation costs of £7.3s.6d. or £7.5s. The cost of the company's one-foot square cast iron pillar amounted to £4.5s. It is not clear how successful the MacFarlane company was in marketing its designs.

By the end of 1931 the Glasgow City Police had been running police box systems of cast iron kiosks, of two successive designs, for almost forty years. At this time the force, now under Sillitoe's command, were to opt for concrete boxes, similar to those introduced into the Metropolitan Police area, albeit initially red in colour.

By the early 1930s the Edinburgh City Police had their own distinctive style of police box designed by the City Architect, Ebenezer Macrae and his assistants. Gavin

Left: Edinburgh City police box at Queenstreet (replaced a previous box demolished by a goods vehicle). Credit: Lothian and Borders Police. Right: Edinburgh Box supporting an air raid siren. Credit: Metropolitan Police Museum.

Exterior and interior shots of Dundee City Police steel beat box. Note the heater and cooker (bottom middle). The worktop on the right opens to reveal a sink. Credit: Tayside Police.

Stamp describes the boxes in his book *Telephone Boxes* as 'a Neoclassical sentry box of great refinement and beauty which harmonises effortlessly with the Classical architecture of the 'Athens of the North''. They were made of cast iron plates bolted together, painted grey, on a concrete base. In later years the colour changed to blue. These boxes contained a writing shelf, a corner seat and stool, a wash–hand basin with running cold water and an electric fire fitted at roof level. They could comfortably accommodate two people.

By the end of 1929 the Dundee Town Council agreed, after a deputation had visited Manchester, Newcastle and Sheffield, that boxes should be recommended for police in the town. In 1933 the Chief Constable of Dundee City Police, W MacDonald, decided to introduce new steel boxes, constructed by Ritchie-Atlas Engineering Co. Ltd., of Glasgow, that he considered superior to the wood, concrete, cast metal or brick used elsewhere in the country. MacDonald's boxes were exhibited at the Dundee Highland Show where a number of chief constables examined them. They were described as being of 'fireproof, neat appearance and clean cut design'.

The steel boxes of Dundee were of three types. The 'section box', larger than the 'beat box' (*described later*), was 12 feet by 4 feet 5 inches by 7 feet 6 inches high and had similar interior equipment, with the addition of a handcuff attachment for securing a prisoner. The section boxes actually replaced police stations (with the exception of the Broughty Ferry beat area).

The beat box, built of heavy gauge steel plates joined with rivets, was 6 feet 4 inches by 4 feet 5 inches and 7 feet 6 inches high with a pyramid shaped roof. The door was also of steel with a special lock. Inside the box the fittings were quite extensive and included a wash-hand basin, a boiling ring and kettle, a tool rack and racks for a bicycle and stretcher. The tool kit included an axe, spanners, a fire extinguisher, insulated pliers, rubber gloves and a five-ton bottle jack. Constables were expected to report on and off duty and make scheduled rings from the beat boxes. They were not permitted to remain in a box for more than two minutes except when writing reports or taking refreshments.

The 'emergency box' was much smaller – 2 feet 9 inches by 2 feet 9 inches by 7 feet 6 inches – than the other two and had no seats. These boxes were used for ringing in and emergencies. All boxes had communication with the police headquarters through the newly designed Ericsson telephone system.

The system finally went into operation in February 1935 and, in due course, Dundee was divided into sub-divisions 'A' and 'B'. The former had three section boxes, twenty-five beat boxes and four emergency boxes and the latter three section boxes, twenty-three beat boxes and twenty-four emergency boxes. The new PA150 switchboard was used in conjunction with the facility.

In the late 1930s the City of London Police erected a few large kiosk type boxes of sheet steel. They were painted green and had an amber flashing light similar to those in use on their pillars.

The use of brick in the construction of police boxes did occur in some areas albeit on a limited scale and often in addition to wooden kiosks. Peterborough City Police installed some brick built boxes, and Tynemouth had its brick boxes and 'section houses'. Another interesting example, operated in Portsmouth, stood at the Portsbridge entrance to Portsea Island with a telephone connection to Cosham Police Station. A brick built box of the Eastbourne County Borough Police adjoined the public toilets – 'Ladies' on one side and 'Gents' on the other.

Brickbuilt box in Portsmouth at Portsbridge entrance to Portsea Island. Credit: Jim Cramer.

Green Street, Eastbourne, 2004, building at the front between public toilets. Previously used as a Police Box.

A most unusual police box located in a stone pillar at the south-east corner of Trafalgar Square went into operation in March 1928. It had cost £479.9s.3d. to rebuild an existing Victorian pillar into the telephone box without affecting the original design, thereby matching the pillar at the opposite corner of the square. Lines from the box, connected to Cannon Row Police Station, New Scotland Yard and Great Scotland Yard, were particularly valuable during meetings and demonstrations to summon assistance if disorder occurred. My recollection, in the 1950s, is of maintaining an up to date list of the registration numbers of stolen cars sent to the box from the station in the hope that they might be seen travelling around the Square.

Concern was expressed in some quarters about there being no easily recognisable colour for kiosks

A recent picture of Trafalgar Square stone kiosk during 2003.

and pillars, which varied from one force to another. In November 1929, at a meeting of chief constables a majority opted for a standard of red with black dado; only two members preferred blue at the time. The colour problem was never really resolved, although in 1948 police generally agreed on blue. This led the Post Office to seek guidance on the shade of blue claiming that they needed to maintain sufficient stocks of paint for their posts.

An article in the *Architects' Journal* in 1931 suggested that the public should be able to immediately recognise a police box anywhere in the country and felt that a kiosk common to all forces would be beneficial. Chief constables generally opposed this view as impractical and felt that this, along with the colour, should be left to the discretion of the local authority.

Although some forces operated with police kiosks of one standard size containing identical facilities, others, like Dundee, operated a system of policing which needed boxes of different sizes depending upon the function they were to perform. In 1929 the Chief Constable of Leeds City Police considered extending his small-scale police box system with a series of small police 'rooms' which would be more practical as substitutes for police stations. Gateshead County Borough Police already operated such a system where, if necessary, a small reserve of policemen could be held at a box. In 1933 the Wolverhampton County Borough Police introduced a box where a sliding gate could partition off an area to hold a prisoner pending his removal to headquarters. Some early kiosks in the London area, for example at Coulsdon and another in the Old Kent Road, had a hand ambulance kept in an adjacent shed.

A kiosk or pillar usually needed to be where it effectively served more than one adjoining beat. The signal light had to be seen for some distance. Consideration also had to be given to the public need in the area. Subsequent urbanisation or redevelopment might require boxes to be resited. Opposition to the selected sites did occur from time to time. In the Metropolitan Police area, for example, opposition by local authorities was countered by the Receiver of the force who claimed that Section 22 Metropolitan Police Act, 1829, that gave the Commissioner authority to erect watch boxes in the nineteenth century, also applied to police boxes. Kensington's local

Wolverhampton Police Box complete with prisoner accommodation c.1933.

authority disputed the claim. The Automobile Association opposed a clause in the Coventry Corporation Bill that empowered the local authority to erect police shelters wherever they wished. The AA felt that they might be built in locations where they could endanger motorists.

While some residents felt safer by having a police box in the vicinity of their home, in the city of Hull, for example, nine residents complained about the decision to site a box near their houses. The Chief Constable's view was that the kiosks were 'by no means inartistic', although the council tended to support the residents. An owner of land in Erith, where a box had been erected by the Metropolitan Police in 1934 on what appeared to be common land, started to remove the box himself after police failed to react with any sense of urgency to his objection.

The telephone equipment varied from the candlestick telephone or the familiar handset to a loudspeaker type microphone device. Whereas the majority of early kiosks incorporated communication equipment supplied independently by a variety of companies, Carter and Co. of Nelson, Lancashire were, by 1927, offering their fully integrated systems of wooden police boxes or iron pillars to forces (otherwise the company could supply fittings for existing boxes). Known as the Carter Micro Police Kiosk or Pillar the signalling system was included, in addition to a loudspeaker telephone for public use. The cost of a pillar with signalling tower was £36, equipping a kiosk £38 and the company even supplied a switchboard for use with their systems at a cost of £380.

Carter do not seem to have been widely successful with their promotion as the Post Office was, by the early 1930s, to monopolise the field with their Ericsson equipment. In 1928 the Chief Constable of the Rochdale County Borough Police did, however, propose siting twenty-two of Carter's kiosks in the town; it seems that the system was also used in Hamilton, Scotland.

In many cases it was possible to send information by telephone to all boxes simultaneously. Keith Rigg recollects in the 1960s all the patrol officers in Eastbourne contacting the station at a scheduled time so that they could receive the information from the station together by way of a 'conference' type of call.

Northampton Borough Police Box with policeman using a candlestick style telephone. Credit: Northamptonshire Police.

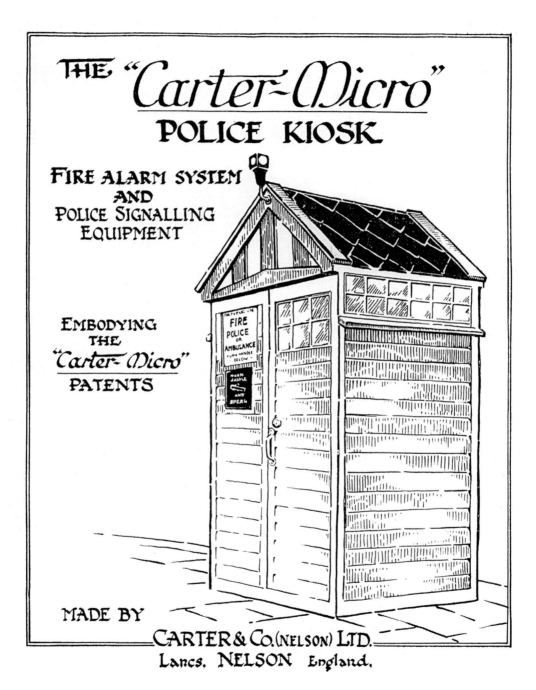

Carter & Co. (Nelson) Ltd publicity.

Signalling lamps and their colours varied from one police area to another – red, white, blue or amber were popular. Earlier lights remained constant when illuminated, whereas later designs incorporated the devices to cause them to flash until a call was answered. The Ministry of Transport complained, in 1933, that flashing red or amber lights were a danger to drivers as they could be confused with traffic lights. After this white lights were generally used, albeit that they could be taken for street lighting. Lamps were often located away from the kiosk or pillar in a highly visible position; for example, the Maidstone Borough Police had signal lights mounted on lamp posts or the corner of buildings allowing them to be seen along more than one street, and Glasgow's red calling lamps were in some cases positioned more than one hundred yards away on walls or tram poles.

Prior to the early 1930s many companies produced communication apparatus for police kiosks and pillars particularly for signalling purposes. Messrs. Stuart & Moore of Ealing had been producing, for some years, a proprietary signalling system, incorporating a red light. Relays for signalling lamps were offered by such companies as The Relay Automatic Telephone Co. Ltd., of Marconi House, The Strand, London, Venner Time Switches Ltd., of Horseferry Road, London, and Messrs. Sterling Telephone and Electric Co. Ltd. The Relay Company described their facility, which was enclosed in a sealed iron case, as causing 'the signal lamp to light when the telephone bell rings and to remain alight until the relay is released'. The company claimed to have an order from the Metropolitan Police. Sterling offered their relays at £4.5s. each or, if in a cast iron box, £12.10s. In the early 1930s the Post Office engineers tested a system known as the Nester Jones police box signal system to ensure its suitability for attachment to their lines; this was a requirement in respect of any proprietary equipment not supplied by the Post Office. Exeter City Police experimented with various companies' signalling devices on their boxes (*described in a previous chapter*).

Although lights remained the preferred means of attracting attention, there were companies offering the alternative of sirens for mounting on police boxes to alert constables to a telephone call. Leach and Co. Ltd. of Artillery Lane, London E.1. was able to supply an electric siren claiming that its distinctive and penetrating noise had an advantage over a flashing lamp. Even the famous Klaxon Company offered, in 1930, to supply suitably adapted sirens for police boxes. Clearly a siren may not have been easily identified in a noisy city street or, in other conditions, may have caused a disturbance to the residents of a neighbourhood. During wartime, however, when the blackout prevailed audible signals often replaced the lights; for example, bells were used to some extent in Bristol and the Metropolitan Police area.

A standard lock secured boxes and constables carried a key to give them access. Retired Metropolitan policeman Tom Long, remembers a comical situation, whilst

Police signal lamp relay publicity.

serving as a sergeant at Ilford, 'One of the older P.C.s made a ring from the box in Cranbrook Rise at about midday. A couple of minutes after making the ring he telephoned again and said he could not open the door and was trapped in the box. The section sergeant made his way there to let the constable out. About a quarter of an hour later the sergeant telephoned the switchboard to say that the wind had blown the door shut when he went in to sort the problem out and they were now both trapped in the box.' A police car crew had to be despatched to release them causing considerable amusement for their colleagues at the station.

Bradford City Police Box key and fob offering a reward to finder if lost.

In some circumstances it was probably preferable to be locked in, rather than locked out of a box, as Brian Goddard of the Metropolitan Police (retired as a Detective Chief Inspector) recalls when, as a probationer constable in the early 1960s, he arrested a drunken young man in Camden High Street, 'I had occasion to arrest a young Irishman who was extremely drunk and incapable – or so I thought. He was tall and strong but in such a state it was very difficult to prop him up and get him to '5N' box. I got him there, put him inside, rang for the 'hurry up wagon', and waited what seemed a lifetime. I couldn't get in the box with him comfortably so held the door slightly open. To my surprise and after a tussle he got the door closed and put the snib down on the dead lock (yale type), leaving me on the pavement – not a happy situation. The next thing I heard was crashing and banging from inside which then gave way to the sound of drumming, singing jolly songs, interspersed with the obscured glass windows being broken as part of the rhythm. It transpired that he wrecked the stool and used the legs to drum on the wooden desktop, etc. No amount of demands pleading to play the game met with a response.' Eventually after causing considerable damage, he was coaxed out with the aid of the sergeant's negotiating skills.

The comfort of the policeman did not appear to be important to the designers of the police kiosks, often containing only a stool and shelf for writing reports. Heating was either absent altogether or consisted of an electric fire (often not working) or radiator. Kiosks would generally have electric lighting although, occasionally, gas was used. Edinburgh's cast iron boxes were renowned for being uncomfortably hot in summer and particularly cold in winter. In the 1930s the Metropolitan Police even had the National Physical Laboratory research and suggest methods of improving the temperature in their boxes.

When retired officers are asked for their recollections of police boxes their memories usually recall how uncomfortable they were. P.C. Ernest Barnett, of the Metropolitan Police, (retired as a Detective Superintendent) remembers, 'Before the Second World War, I was stationed at Chiswick, 'F' Div., and part of our ground was a section of the Great West Road where they had installed a police box. Memory tells me it was made of concrete. In those days the beat officer took his thirty-minute meal break in the box and very cold it was. One day one of our brighter young men took along a portable electric fire, plugged it into the light socket and blew the whole system.'

Retired P.C. Geoff Lawrence, remembers the boxes in north London in the 1950s, '34 Y was in Green Lanes, Haringey, N.4., outside the Oakwood Laundry and served both 'N' and 'Y' divisions. It became so cold and soaked

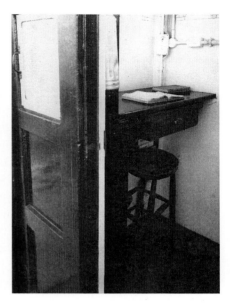

The interior of a Metropolitan Police Box. Credit: Metropolitan Police.

with condensation inside that I used to light a bonfire of matchsticks, etc. in a tin used as an ashtray to have a warm up. There was no heater available in any of the boxes, despite the fact that one was fitted. It became known that an electrically minded officer had managed to get the heater going in a box which was situated by the Archway near Highgate and we often went there for a warm up in 6N area car during a cold night.'

Although not a place of comfort the box could provide a certain amount of safety for the policeman. Retired Detective Chief Inspector Bill Hose remembers as a young constable in east London in the 1960s being called to a serious disturbance in a public house in Grove Road, Bow. Confident that he could sort out the problem alone he entered the premises, but was immediately confronted by customers very hostile to the presence of the law. Hasty retreat was the only sensible answer if he was not to be attacked. The nearby police box fortunately provided temporary safety from where he could summon assistance.

Boxes were not immune to damage from motor vehicle collisions, as they were often positioned at junctions where accidents were more likely. An example in Beverley High Road, Hull in 1933 saw extensive damage caused to a kiosk by a lorry. Retired Chief Inspector John Brewer had the opposite memory – a car being 'struck by a flying police box' during demolition, as it was loaded, by crane, on to the back of a lorry in northwest London.

Although P.C. Hose found the police box a safe haven, this was not P.C. Andrewartha's experience in August 1937. Whilst taking his refreshments at about 5.40 p.m. in No. 10 Box on 'R' Division, situated in Plumstead Road, Woolwich, a loaded trolleybus struck and completely demolished the box and the stool on which he had been sitting. Both he and a colleague, standing outside at the time, were detained in St Nicholas Hospital for many weeks with serious injuries.

Police boxes were important during the war when many were continuously manned with the air raid sirens mounted on the top or on tall poles alongside. (In London, after the war, some sirens formed part of the Thames flood warning system.) They were often protected by sandbags and brick walls. R. Howard, of the Sheffield City Police, recalls that in the war years the public kept a close watch on the police box lamps in the belief that when the lamp was illuminated an air raid was imminent.

Retired Police Constable Winterflood, who served at Hendon Police Station on Metropolitan's 'S' Division, during the war years, recounts, 'When I was transferred to Hendon Station in 1938 the 'Box System' had been in operation about three years, and very unpopular it was with the rank and file. At outbreak of war certain boxes were designated as sub-air raid warning stations and cosily wrapped round on all sides with layers of sandbags, but not on the roof, which was fitted with a system to be manually operated inside the box by a lever or was it a button? I forget.

Police Box in Beverley High Road, Hull, struck by a lorry in 1933. Credit: Hull City Archives.

Air raid siren alongside a Police Box in London. Credit: Metropolitan Police.

These boxes were manned twenty-four hours a day by a P.C. who was not permitted to stay inside (not that he wanted to anyway; it was too damned uncomfortable) but had to stand outside until summoned inside by the flashing blue lamp on the roof. If the message was the first warning of an impending air raid, the P.C. had to remain inside to press the lever (or button) for two minutes to set up the up and down wail of the system if the red alert came up. He had to remain until notified by S.E. (Edgware Police Station) to sound the 'all clear'. On one occasion in the box an officer was struck on the steel helmet he was wearing when an anti-aircraft shell pierced the roof to this box.'

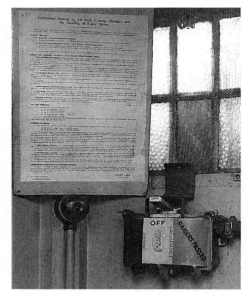

Interior equipment for operating the air raid siren on a London Police Box. Credit: Metropolitan Police.

Retired Metropolitan Police Constable Fred Hughes recollects being posted to Box 32 in Green Street, Upton Park, on a beautiful clear night around 1940 when his attention was drawn to an aircraft circling above him. The aeroplane suddenly released all its bombs. They seemed to be dropping towards him. He made for the nearby police box and crouched down on the floor for shelter. Fortunately for him the bombs fell on East Ham Manor a short distance away. Feeling safe and relieved he rose from the floor, but just as he did so the telephone rang. The sudden noise gave him such a shock that he thought a bomb had struck and his time was up.

Forces continually tried to encourage public use of the boxes with limited success. Notices on the outside of many boxes and posts made it clear that they were available to use in order to seek assistance. The Chief Constable of the Leeds City Police, keen to ensure the proper education in the use of the system, arranged for a large sized model to be constructed for instructional purposes during police visits to schools. The Metropolitan Police took stands, during 1930s, at Radiolympia and the Ideal Home Exhibitions at Olympia where thousands of pamphlets were distributed to visitors, and a police box on show was connected up to the local police station for public use.

Retired Police Sergeant Roland Swanborough, serving at Acton Police Station, remembers being posted to the Metropolitan Police Stand at the Ideal Home Exhibition, 'My duties there, shared with three P.S.s from other divisions, were to do our best to interest people in the usefulness of the boxes, one of which, on the stand, was connected

A Metropolitan Police exhibition stand. Credit: Metropolitan Police.

to Hammersmith, 'F' Division, and persuade them to make a call on that line to learn how easily it worked. A pleasant change from Early Turn or Night Duty for a month.'

The constable's ability from inside the box to observe the public outside, without their being aware, could be an advantage. This unexpected witness could surprise those engaged in crime or disorder nearby.

Relying on the ability to see out would not always be a good idea as Police Constable Salmon of the Metropolitan Police, discovered when he was assigned to a peak hour traffic point at Elmers End Road in Beckenham, 'It was tipping it down with freezing sleet and snow. I entered the box for a little comfort feeling thoroughly miserable and very wet. With practice it was possible to sit on

POLICE TELEPHONE
FREE
FOR USE OF
PUBLIC
ADVICE AND ASSISTANCE
OBTAINABLE IMMEDIATELY

OFFICERS AND CARS
RESPOND TO
URGENT CALLS

PULL TO OPEN

The notice displayed on boxes encouraging use by the public.

the writing desk and by thrusting the hands into your pockets, putting the feet on the stool and drawing the body up into a ball, removing the helmet and thrusting the chin into the tunic a certain comfort was offered. By bending the neck at an acute angle I was able to peep out of the windows and keep an eye on the traffic position.' Unfortunately P.C. Salmon's cosiness was soon disturbed when the traffic came to sudden halt; he exited the box in a panic, leaving his helmet behind and losing his white traffic gauntlets in the process. The reason for his alarm – his inspector's car had been caught up in the jam!

The kiosk also provided a place where the constable could write a report in reasonable comfort. Frederick Crawley, when Chief Constable of Newcastle-upon-Tyne, highlighted the problems existing prior to police boxes, 'It was the custom for Police to stand in all kinds of inclement weather, sometimes with rain pouring off their capes, jostled by the public, etc. in an endeavour to enter a report in the pocket book. In other times they would creep away to some mews where there was a good fire in a cabmen's harness room.'

Boxes on the outskirts of the Northampton County Borough Police area, in common with many other places, were large enough to provide toilet facilities and a gas ring to prepare meals. By 1955 the borough had twenty-two boxes and nineteen pillars in use. Ernest Croxson writes about police boxes on the outer beats of Norwich City (*The Police History Society Journal*, 2000), 'These were warmed by a small electric ring and tea or coffee was distributed by car in enamel cans. The man delivering the tea or coffee often tried to help by switching the heating ring on and putting the drink on it to keep warm. Unfortunately if the beat man was delayed the drink would be boiled for a long period until he arrived and was not fit to drink.'

Bicycles were often used by policemen, particularly in the outer areas of the boroughs and cities, either as a means of patrolling or for conveying an officer to his beat. Provision of secure storage for the cycles, within the box or adjacent to it, was often made, although not always. Keith Rigg remembers, in the 1960s, that the brick built box at Seaside, in Eastbourne had only an outside cycle rack at the rear. After parading at the sub-divisional station about a mile away, the beat officer would take one of the official police bikes and cycle to the box from where he would commence his patrol. The cycle would be chained up in the rack but, fearful that the 'locals' would steal the valves, they were removed from the tyres and left in the box. On return at refreshment time valves would be replaced and the tyres pumped up for the return journey to the police station. These procedures were followed on any occasion the cycles were left at the box.

Training recruits, new to the service, required them to be familiarised with the police box and its facilities. At the Metropolitan Police training establishments the exercises for trainees were often staged in the vicinity of the school's police box where a realistic scene could be set up. A 'traffic accident', or other mock incident, would require the student to deal with it making any necessary calls for assistance through the telephone in the box, watched critically by other recruits.

A number of ideas were put forward to extend the usefulness of the box. In September 1934, F. S. James, Sheffield's Chief Constable, suggested that in outlying districts 'public utility boxes' should have, as well as the police function, a public telephone, postage stamp dispenser and post box. In 1933 Atlas Ritchie Engineering claimed to have developed a 'signature clock' so that a policeman's visit to the box would be automatically registered without a 'ring in' being necessary. A Nottingham constable thought that every box should be fitted with a telegraphic tape machine so that urgent messages could be sent simultaneously to all kiosks. These suggestions do not appear to have materialised, although the 1960s did see the short-term introduction of the 'Robofone' by the City of London Police whereby officers could dictate their reports over the telephone at a box on to the machine at the police station.

By the 1920s the kiosk was not the sole preserve of the police authorities and the General Post Office; the Automobile Association and Royal Automobile Club were locating boxes on major roads for use by their patrolmen and organisation members. Even the British Red Cross installed a wooden kiosk as a first aid post on the Kingston By-Pass with equipment to deal with accidents and casualties.

As late as 1937, with the Post Office system in widespread use, the Chief Constable of Nottingham City Police still contemplated the installation of a hundred proprietary police and fire brigade pillars in the outer parts of the city. One hundred old call points already serviced the inner city. Standard Telephones and Cables and the Automatic Electric Company submitted estimates of £10,608 and £9,733 respectively, for a Gamewell system.

Police posts did not allow the same privacy for the constable's telephone conversations as the kiosk. Peter Walton, serving as a constable at West End Central in London (retired as a Deputy Assistant Commissioner), recollects that newspaper reporters would occasionally hang around near the post at Piccadilly Circus in the hope that, when the light flashed for the constable on duty there to attend to a call, they would gain information about the location of an incident from his conversations. They could then take a cab to the scene to get their story.

Trying to call for assistance from a police post whilst holding a struggling prisoner was not a particularly easy task. Although there is no evidence of similar facilities in this country, the police posts in the Georgetown area of Washington in the United States were apparently fitted with 'prisoner rings' to which an arrested person could be handcuffed whilst the police officer awaited transport.

As a general rule the county constabularies did not introduce police box systems into the rural areas, consequently alternative forms of communication were necessary. Police houses in the villages, and borough outskirts, often provided a link with the station. Following the war, call point facilities, for example in Northampton and Peterborough, were attached to police houses, and in the Sussex Police a small police office was often located between two houses accessible from either. When necessary other police officers on patrol could use the facilities.

Retired Police Constable Ian Ewence, of the Surrey Police, recollects the 1960s force schedules for using the public telephone kiosks for communication with the station when on patrol. Officers were required to attend particular payphone boxes on their beat at nominated times to await a possible call from the station and would, if necessary, remain there for fifteen minutes. Successful communication was in jeopardy if a member of the public was already using the telephone. In some instances, where there were no public boxes, nominated private or business telephones were used. Similar systems operated in most counties throughout the country, and provided a method whereby constables could be located at particular times.

Although this research concentrates on this country, across the world police call points have been used even, it appears, as far afield as Port Moresby in Papua New Guinea. Certainly there was a system of pillars in Frankfurt, Germany, in the 1980s, and, more recently, in New York emergency posts were seen. So a wealth of information still remains to be unearthed both here and abroad by the enthusiast.

Southampton constable writing at a PA1 post c.1943. Credit: Hampshire Constabulary.

Police pillar in Frankfurt, Germany, 1980s.

Chapter 8

THE DYING DAYS OF
THE POLICE BOX (1960-2011)

Police boxes have ranged from wall units, pillars or wooden huts, barely large enough to take one person, to structures capable of accommodating a small reserve of policemen. The early twentieth century saw their initial, rather complex, communication equipment give way to simpler facilities based on a telephone with suitable signalling devices. Eventual Post Office standardisation of this equipment ensured the continued widespread success of the schemes throughout the 1950s, by which time a large proportion of the major built-up areas of the country had boxes of one form or another in operation. Rural areas, falling within the borough or city boundaries where systems had been introduced, were usually served by them. However, the logistics involved in implementing schemes in the remote areas of the county constabularies had generally made it impractical and uneconomic to do so.

Even as early as 1927 some were questioning the effect wireless would have on the need for police boxes as a means of communication from the street. Frederick Crawley, then Newcastle's Chief Constable, confident of the police box's future observed in response, 'Assuming that the time may come when Police will be moving about with wireless apparatus in the helmets, always admitting that their reception is by code or a form of attunment which would prevent the general public from receiving same, we still maintain that the Police Box System is not affected thereby for the three following reasons:

  a. The principle of decentralisation of policing enabling Police to start on their beat instead of at a distant police station would not be helped thereby.
  b. The public would not have any means of call as is provided by the Police Boxes.
  c. Police would have no place for writing their reports as is similarly provided by the Boxes.'

Needless to say the boxes went from strength to strength for many years ahead until even Crawley's optimism proved unsustainable.

The 1960s were to see the beginning of the end for the police box when forces, throughout the United Kingdom, began seriously to introduce personal radio systems. Radio would no longer be the sole preserve of the police car and motorcycle; foot patrols would carry their own means of communication at all times. The late 1960s saw the county borough forces absorbed into the constabularies, sometimes resulting in inconsistencies in respect of street communication from one newly merged borough to another. Any thoughts of extending or upgrading these ageing systems would be costly and uneconomical (some forces were still operating with old wooden kiosks that had seen better days). Maintenance and line rental costs were substantial and finance could be better spent elsewhere.

Other means of communication were overwhelming and the police box could not compete. It made little economic sense to retain a scheme merely for casual use by constables. In any event, in some areas, foot patrols were giving way to motor patrols, and new 'unit beat policing' schemes, along with so called 'panda cars', had to some extent reinforced the obsolescence of the police box. A box system no longer in regular use would no doubt attract the vandals. The time was right for their retirement and an extension of more modern methods.

The public would hardly notice the disappearance of the police boxes as they were rarely using them. When they did the call would generally be of a routine non-urgent nature. Usually the householder or, alternatively, a nearby neighbour had a telephone in their home. Failing this a public telephone kiosk (unfortunately often vandalised) would not be too far away. In conjunction with these readily available facilities, the '999' service provided that rapid link with the emergency services (Fire brigades had already abandoned street alarm systems and were relying on the service). In addition people were more mobile with their own means of transport for use when they were in difficulty.

The police box could have little impact on crime with the criminal generally using a motor vehicle, sometimes stolen, to commit offences. Wireless now provided the most effective means for passing information and mobilising police.

'Ringing in' had become an unnecessary supervisory chore and, in London, the schedules were, in due course, substituted by the instruction, 'Each officer will maintain regular radio contact with the station'. Officers were becoming more discerning, and few would savour taking lunch in an old, cold (too hot in summer), unhygienic kiosk. Many years before cynics had probably already observed that allocating a building between two public toilets in Eastbourne as a police box, or siting one beside a smelly overflowing urinal in Wornington Road, west London, showed the esteem in which the famous British bobbie was actually held!

The ordinary policeman would hardly be mourning the passing of the police boxes. Retired Constable Cal Gilbert of the Coventry City Police, writing to the *Coventry*

Evening Telegraph, in February 1989, some years after their demise, probably sums up the general feeling when he suggested that they should have been 'consigned to the Black Museum'. He went on to give his reasons, 'Indelibly printed on my memory are recollections of balancing on a high stool at a sloping desk at about 2 a.m. trying to hold a flask and sandwiches on a 3 inch wide shelf. Many times the vacuum flask fell, depriving me of a much-needed hot drink when there was no prospect of getting another that night.

The boxes had no heating. On severe winter nights icicles would hang from the interior and, if it was less cold but wet, moisture would stream down the walls.

On cold nights to retain some body heat during a 30 minute meal break it was necessary to sit with greatcoat collar turned up, helmet back to front and cape wrapped around the legs.'

Whereas in some areas kiosks and pillars were rapidly removed completely, elsewhere they were gradually reduced in number. The 1965 formation of the Mid-Anglia Constabulary, for example, saw the Chief Constable review the systems in the two main cities, Peterborough and Cambridge, that had been absorbed into the force. Seven kiosks and eight pillars remained in Peterborough when it was decided to dispense with five of the pillars; the annual saving was estimated at £305. Only 102 public calls had been made during the whole of the previous year. In Cambridge in 1957 there had been a total of six kiosks and twenty-nine pillars; by 1967 they had been reduced to four kiosks and one pillar by the new force. In Dorset the constabulary phased out its eight posts and one kiosk in the town of Poole in 1964, saving £561 in the first year and £1,425 in subsequent years.

The removal of a scheme from a small provincial town was a relatively painless exercise, whereas in the large cities it proved to be a major costly project. By 1952 Bradford City Police had 104 boxes in the city centre and outer districts; by 1960 they were down to forty-seven. The late 1960s saw most of the boxes withdrawn, remembered by retired Police Sergeant Paul Dixon, serving in the force as a constable at the time, as, '... to say the least spartan, comprising little more than a sink with cold water and a small gas ring or electric stove'. With the demise of Bradford's old boxes a few, substantial, purpose-built 'beat boxes' were introduced to cater for the newly implemented unit beat policing scheme. In the Midlands the Coventry City Police had, by June 1969, removed most of the telephones from their wooden kiosks when the decision was made to dismantle them, apart from a few in the city centre. Similar abandoning of schemes can be found in large and small forces throughout the country.

As early as 1958 in London, where the Metropolitan Police had the country's most extensive scheme totalling about 750 kiosks and pillars, there was a decision to remove ninety-six kiosks and three posts. Although lightweight motorcycle patrols, with wireless communication had been introduced on divisions, this was not felt at

Destruction of the Metropolitan Police Boxes. Credit: Metropolitan Police.

the time to provide sufficient reason for reducing the number of boxes more drastically. It seems that a total of 105 were actually removed in 1960, with the bulk of the system remaining intact.

Trials with personal radios started in 1965 on four Metropolitan sub-divisions, and by 1969, the final sub-divisions had been completed with a total of 4525 radios having been allocated throughout the force. The demolition of the remaining kiosks and posts proceeded, apart from about twelve that were to remain. Additionally a few others were to be retained temporarily for particular reasons; for example, two boxes were left in parts of outer London until public telephone kiosks had been installed nearby. The last of the final twelve operational kiosks, located at the Barnet By-pass, was finally demolished in 1980.

Removal costs in London were estimated to be in the region of £80 to £100 for each box, thus amounting to a total of some £68,000; the long term saving on maintenance costs, however, came to about £60,000 each year. The extensive demolition programme required the careful co-ordination of the various services – G.P.O., electricity board and the demolition contractor – as it was felt that a box could not be left in public view without a telephone operating. Although most were in public places some one hundred were on private land, and over 230 had air raid sirens associated with them, available as a warning system in the event of an anticipated nuclear attack.

Destruction or disposal of the unwanted structures all over the country usually fell to the contractor. The old wooden boxes obviously made good firewood. In London, however, many of the two and a half-ton structures had to be broken up on site, although some did have temporary respite in a police box 'graveyard' at Hendon. It seems that Southend-on-Sea's metal pillars were dumped in an unused police motor vehicle inspection pit and cemented over. What will an archæologist make of a find like this in a few centuries time?

The saviour of some Police posts – P.C. Peter Wright, 1972. Credit: Metropolitan Police.

Although the 1960s and 70s saw the widespread removal of kiosks and pillars throughout the United Kingdom three notable exceptions were Edinburgh (Lothian and Borders Police 1975), Glasgow (Strathclyde Police 1975) and the City Police area of London, where substantial systems were retained for many years.

The 1960s saw Edinburgh lose its telephone pillars, and subsequently a more flexible style of policing, introduced in the 1970s, saw a decision to phase-out the remaining part of the kiosk system. Although a number were removed a network of beat boxes remained (some with air raid sirens) for casual use. The saviour of many of these cast iron structures was reputedly the high cost and difficulty in removing them (although in May, 2000 one was actually stolen and later recovered). In 1995 about thirty-five boxes were sold by auction, still leaving a substantial number, with many then given listed building status by Historic Scotland. Recently one of the removed kiosks appeared for sale on the auction site 'ebay' with a minimum price-tag of £4000 placed on it.

Some of Edinburgh's kiosks were taken over by the California Coffee Company who, it is claimed, spent £20,000 each on their conversion into coffee stalls. Stalls are still in use, albeit with a different company. Others were converted, for a short time, into Police Information Boxes by the Lothian and Borders Police, and another was reputedly to be used as a ticket kiosk by Lothian Buses. Plans are currently underway, to bring some boxes back into limited operational use in Grassmarket and other busy parts of the city; this has already happened in Marchmont.

Left: Edinburgh's Police Information Box, 2004. Credit: Martin Holmes. Right: Edinburgh Police Box converted into a coffee stall, 2010.

In 1972 sixty-three of Glasgow's kiosks remained. They had been reduced to eleven by 1993 when the decision to abandon the system completely was made. Only one box, resited in Buchanan Street, was to be retained. Fortunately the Civil Defence and Emergency Service Preservation Trust, along with the Glasgow Building Preservation Trust, came to the rescue and have brought a few of the neglected boxes back to their former glory. Four are now listed.

Glasgow's box became a temporary work of modern art in 1997 when the artist, Ann Shaw, took part in a public art project on behalf of the Glasgow Gallery of Modern Art. She painted the box white and covered it in coloured spots. One of the city's restored boxes is serving coffee amusingly described as 'Coppuccino', and another is on loan to the Kent Police Museum.

Other than Edinburgh few kiosks have survived intact in public places. Good examples do, however, remain at Sandside in Scarborough, in Sheffield outside the Town Hall, at Newtown Linford in Leicestershire (apparently moved from North Kilworth in 1952) and Almondbury near Huddersfield. The concrete kiosk in Newport, Gwent, adorned with a painted *Doctor Who* scarf, is sadly in need of substantial renovation.

Police kiosks have occasionally been retained in situ, and subsequently used for other purposes. Brighton's sizeable pier-side structure became a sandwich bar. In some places Traffic Wardens took over an abandoned town centre box, and a brick built structure in Albert Parade, Eastbourne is currently being brought back for use by Police Community Support Officers (PCSOs). The proud looking hollowed stone

Left: Brighton's sizeable pier-side structure, now a sandwich bar, 2004. Right: Coventry's Box is now a garden shed, 2004. Credit: West Midlands Police Museum.

The surviving Police Box at Sandside Scarborough. Credit:Yorkshire Regional Newspapers Ltd.

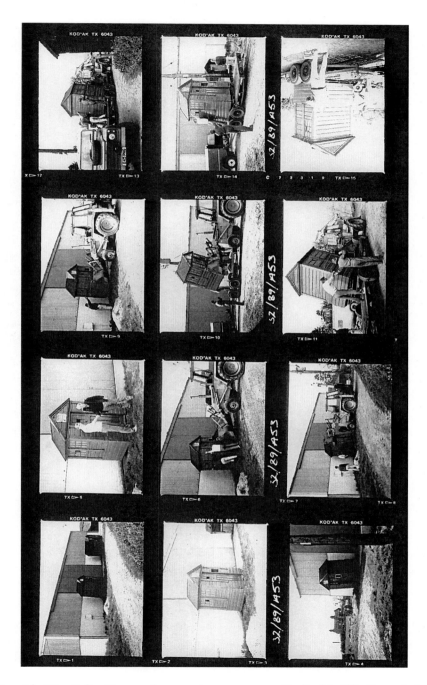

Norwich City Police Box on the move in recent years. Credit: Norfolk Constabulary.

Left: Police Box at Force Training School, Bishopgarth, Wakefield, West Yorkshire. Credit: West Yorkshire Police. Right: Sergeant Richard Farmery at the Metropolitan Police Training School Box, 2004.

police box on Trafalgar Square (once described grandly as the smallest police station) has been reduced to a street cleaners' store for brushes and other equipment. Two London kiosks have long retired from 'traffic duty' at the Blackwall Tunnel.

Some kiosks undertook other roles after removal from the street. A large wooden box from Bradford eventually took up residence as the scorer's box at a local cricket ground, and in Coventry, one finished up as a payment kiosk for entry to a local railway visitor centre. Many timber kiosks had second lives as garden sheds, with a few possibly still providing good service to amateur gardeners in parts of the country; the purchasing price for an enthusiast in Coventry was £5. A farmer in Norfolk is still believed to be keeping a Norwich City box in his farmyard. Efforts, however, to locate a Kings Lynn box, that was apparently moved to a local housing estate, have been unsuccessful. Two abandoned kiosks, previously used by Thames Water, survive at their Crossness site; they look suspiciously like the later design of the Metropolitan Police kiosk.

Over the years there have always been kiosks, or other small buildings, designed, or adapted, for specific policing tasks and not part of a police box scheme. A raised circular traffic control box in the centre of Market Place in Durham gave the police constable responsible for controlling the nearby traffic signals, a good view of the situation, and proper shelter whilst undertaking the task. A windscreen could be moved around to protect him from the weather as required. From 1909 an observation box in Hyde Park, with telephone connections to Scotland Yard and other relevant locations, including a wooden police box at Speakers' Corner, was used by the Metropolitan Police to monitor the situation during demonstrations. Marble Arch was also used by the force, as was a small police station located in Wellington Arch, for constables undertaking traffic duty at Hyde Park Corner.

Police premises or museums house a few kiosks lucky enough to have avoided destruction. Although there is a later design of the Metropolitan Police box at their Hendon Training School, the only surviving genuine *Doctor Who* style concrete kiosk is now at the National Tramway Museum at Crich, Derbyshire. A recent renovation, by Ivor Parnham Building Services, has brought it back to its former glory. The Avoncroft Museum in Bromsgrove provides the visitor with a selection of kiosks and pillars on display. The recent unexpected discovery, and rescue from an original city site in Glasgow, of an old cast iron kiosk is prized by the curator of the Police Museum, who proudly displays it there in restored condition. Even its original telephone was handed in by a local resident. Similarly the recently restored wooden kiosk, that stood in Old Market Square, Nottingham, is now at the force headquarters. A garden shed, donated by a local Coventry resident, is under restoration to its original police box status by the Coventry Transport Museum.

Market Place Traffic Box in Durham c1952 with PC Tommy Stevenson on duty. Note damage to roof of box. Credit: Photographic Archive, Beamish Museum.

The sole surviving genuine 'Doctor Who' concrete Metropolitan Police Box at the National Tramway Museum.

A concrete Glasgow City Police Box sits alongside a timber Coventry City Box at the Avoncroft Museum in Bromsgrove, Worcestershire, 2004.

The City of London Police scheme consisted mainly of police posts with very few kiosks. The old green posts that seem to have been installed in the late 1920s were replaced in 1965 by standard PA3 style pillars. Not until 1988 did the force substitute these sixty-five posts with, at the time, a free-call telephone facility to the police headquarters from public telephone kiosks located near the abandoned sites. A few posts still remain in the City with preservation orders on them, albeit painted in dark blue rather than the more authentic light blue previously used.

Posts generally seem to have had a slightly better survival rate than kiosks. There are two remaining Metropolitan Police posts – at Piccadilly Circus (the original strangely disappeared a few years ago and was not replaced by an authentic Met post) and Grosvenor Square near the United States Embassy. The last one to be removed in the Met area was outside Chelsea Football Club. A PA1 is placed outside Rochester Police Station in Kent, to assist visitors communicate with the station.

Pillars of the standard designs are to be found in the hands of private collectors, who can spend many hours carefully restoring them. Rodney Marshall, a street furniture enthusiast, plans to connect his PA1 and PA3 pillars to a small switchboard in his home, and Laurence Rudolf in north London is continually trying to locate authentic fittings for his prized possessions. For those less inclined to undertake renovation themselves the professionals at Unicorn Restorations, noted for their work on G.P.O. telephone kiosks, will arrange restoration at a price. Unfortunately the fate of the eighteen 'retired' Metropolitan Police posts that were purchased by Police Constable Peter Wright, of Southwalk, in 1972, and initially kept in his garden and garage, is unknown. However, retired P.C. Donald Sinclair's post, positioned beside the front door of his Bromley home, was ideally located for deliveries of post or milk.

Although the London police box had always struck a chord with model makers, it was the 1960s fictional BBC television series *Doctor Who* (now back on TV) that created a continuing interest in what became known as the 'Tardis' (Time and Relative Dimension In Space). A failed appeal in recent years by the Metropolitan Police against the Patent Office's decision to grant trade mark rights to the BBC in respect of the box, means that they [the BBC] can continue to use the image on their Doctor Who products without payment. Publicity material usually portrays the police box and, not unexpectedly, the entrance to Lands End's Doctor Who exhibition is in the form of an exceptionally large Tardis.

Replicas of the iconic London police box have, over the years, been produced as money-boxes, teapots, birdboxes, salt and pepper pots and a variety of other objects. A replica kiosk is located at Wetherby Police Station in Yorkshire, and a company produced almost 'life size' copies for sale to the public. You can even have your bedroom wardrobe in the shape of a police box if you are so inclined!

Ian Ewence is the proud owner of a scale model presented to his father, Bob, on retirement, who saw the boxes *in* as an apprentice on the design team in London and *out* as the Senior Building Surveyor responsible for their removal. A colleague of the author, Inspector Eddie George, would surprise his retiring staff with a bottle of whisky hidden in a replica police box meticulously crafted by himself for the purpose. Tony Purbrick, in Cape Cod in the United States, has recently sold many of the items from his small private police collection, which he claimed included the smallest authentic scale

Retired pillar in garden of Donald Sinclair's home in Bromley. The milkman delivered milk bottles in it!

Tony Purbrick's replica Police Box. Credit: Anthony C. Purbrick.

model of a Metropolitan Police kiosk, with all the accessories and fittings. So, although the box has almost disappeared, it is not forgotten.

In America police call boxes are also struggling for survival. Washington DC abandoned its call points on the arrival of the 911 emergency facility in 1976. (Interestingly call points of specially polished brass were apparently positioned in front of the White House, and at Union Station to communicate President Roosevelt's arrival in the city). In 2000 a survey discovered that over 1100 of the abandoned fire and police call posts were still in place in Washington DC. These are now being restored as 'artistic icons' by the Cultural Tourism Department; in 2002/3 700 were stripped and prepared for the artwork to be installed in the cupboard space. Until recent years, although not confirmed, the city of San Francisco was reputedly operating a system.

A disused US police post in Washington DC, USA, 2005.

Readers will probably question the author's state of mind when told he is on the look-out for anything resembling a police box system when on holiday, albeit without success. In 2010 in Santa Cruz de Tenerife a solitary S.O.S. pillar was spotted; in Rome, in 2011, kiosks housing security staff near the government buildings, took his eye, along with one used by the Municipal Police in another part of the city. Maybe a visit to Japan to see Tokyo's 'koban' or miniature police stations, or Hong Kong's traffic police service boxes will be in order? A police kiosk in Cathedral Square, Christchurch, New Zealand, staffed by volunteers, would hardly be an excuse to go there? The campuses of many American universities have emergency call points connected directly to police headquarters for student safety, as have Boston's city parks for visitor safety.

Police box schemes, in their original form, have now completely disappeared in this country and probably elsewhere. We are now left with the reintroduction of kiosks, or other call points, either specifically for police security purposes, or for public use in respect of safety, crime reporting, information or assistance. In the 1990s, for example, a new police box, copying the old design, with up

S.O.S. pillar in Santa Cruz de Tenerife, 2010.

to date communications equipment, including CCTV, was erected outside the busy Earl's Court Underground Station, London, as a crime prevention measure. Similarly, where police have a high profile security responsibility, there is a place for a modern highly visible kiosk to accommodate them; examples exist at the rear of Downing Street and outside parliament.

The London Borough of Haringey, with police support, introduced two easily identifiable kiosks in busy parts of the borough where contact could be made with local police officers at particular times for advice and assistance. Many of the 'it seemed like a good idea at the time' projects, like the conversion of boxes into Police Information Boxes in Edinburgh, do not seem to have survived. The Royal Parks Constabulary's (this force was absorbed into the Metropolitan Police in 2004) SOS Call Point scheme, introduced in Hyde Park in the 1996, designed to assist visitors to the park if they were in difficulty, was apparently abandoned some years ago. In 2005 Sir Ian Blair, the Metropolitan Police Commissioner, officially opened a police 'pavilion' at Piccadilly Circus, where staff could

Modern Police kiosk at Wood Green, London Borough of Haringey, 2004.

assist the many visitors to the area. This is no longer there. The success or otherwise of a similar facility, introduced by the Strathclyde Police in Glasgow, has not been established.

The Avon and Somerset Constabulary have recently subscribed to a number of touch-screen information points, sited at various locations, including a few in supermarkets, from where police can be contacted. In Cambridgeshire there are similar points in hospitals available to victims of assault or serious accident. The City of London Police have a telephone link for the residents of a local housing estate. The Hertfordshire Police's multimedia kiosk in Watford town centre allows the public to

Modern Police Box on Horse Guard's Parade, London, 2003.

make contact on-line or by telephone, as does a system at Fishergate in Preston, Lancashire. Whether these, and other locally introduced police information points, will actually survive has yet to be seen.

Police stations, open for a restricted number of hours each day, have a facility outside providing a direct link for the public to a control centre during the hours of closure. The South Wales Police have, for example, a modern interactive system at the Mumbles Police Station for such use. All our motorways have telephone posts at regular intervals to enable motorists to contact the control rooms in an emergency, with similar systems operating in road tunnels and other major highways. A Help Point emergency system operates at London Underground stations.

The innovative police box systems of the 1920s and 1930s, welcomed by so many chief constables, rose rapidly to transform many aspects of British policing. No new policing method had previously been so universally accepted by forces throughout the whole country and, undoubtedly, increased the liaison between forces, albeit with some rivalry. Systems fell from grace completely in the 1960s, and their return for day-to-day operational policing, as is sometimes speculated in the press, is unlikely.

Although police boxes are long gone, speak to any retired officer who worked with them, and he will probably have an interesting anecdote to tell. The author recently mentioned this book to an ex-colleague, Mike Turner, and he immediately, without prompting, relayed his amusing experience as a young constable at Golders Green in London. As he opened the door to enter the box he found it difficult to comprehend why daylight was coming in through the rear. The reason the whole back wall had disappeared!

Clearly there is still scope for more research into, and analysis of, this important aspect of policing; perhaps considering its social and economic impact, or even whether schemes had actually been productive in reducing crime. Examining specific areas of the country in more detail would prove interesting for the local historian, and provide valuable documented information for local museums and archives. Others may find the technical side of the systems a fulfilling project. This book will provide a sound base for future research and will have dispelled the public's perception that the police boxes were cosy resting-places for tired or lazy policemen. We should now, however, accept that the police box has had its day and let it rest in peace.

Chief Superintendent Eddie Gleeson, the wise and experienced head of the huge Communications Branch at New Scotland Yard, throughout the period in the 1980s when major computerisation of the message handling systems were impacting on the force, was not prone to fits of nostalgia. On his office desk, however, stood a rather battered blue miniature Dinky toy police box. Why was it there? Maybe the occasional casual glance at the 'little fellow' subtly reminded him of those less complicated days in police communications!

APPENDIX A

British Police Forces – Proposed or Installed Police Box Systems between 1923 and 1939 (Y)

Police Force	**Year of Initial Merger, Renaming or Amalgamation of a Force after 1923#**	**Adopted or Proposed a Police Box System between 1923 & 1931+**	**Adopted or Proposed a GPO PA1 Call System between 1932 & 1939+ K=Kiosk, P=Pillar**
ENGLAND			
Bedfordshire County	1966	–	–
Bedford Borough	1947	–	Y
Luton Borough	1947	–	Y – 12K/18P
Berkshire County	1968	–	–
New Windsor Borough	1947	–	–
Reading County Borough	1968	Y	Y – 32 K/P
Buckinghamshire County	1968	–	–
Chepping Wycombe Borough	1947	–	Y
Cambridgeshire County	1965	–	–
Cambridge City	1965	Y	–
Isle of Ely Constabulary	1965	–	–
Cheshire County	–	–	Y★
Birkenhead County Borough	1967	–	Y (in 1943)
Chester City	1949	–	–
Congleton Borough	1947	–	–
Hyde Borough	1947	–	Y
Macclesfield Borough	1947	Y	Y – 16 P
Stalybridge Borough	1947	Y	–
Stockport County Borough	1967	Y	Y
Wallasey County Borough	1967	Y	Y (in 1940)

Police Force	Year of Initial Merger, Renaming or Amalgamation of a Force after 1923 #	Adopted or Proposed a Police Box System between 1923 & 1931 +	Adopted or Proposed a GPO PA1 Call System between 1932 & 1939 + K=Kiosk, P=Pillar
ENGLAND			
Cornwall County	1967	–	–
Penzance Borough	1943	–	–
Cumberland County	1963	–	–
Carlisle City	1963	–	–
Derbyshire County	1967	–	–
Chesterfield Borough	1947	Y	Y
Derby County Borough	1967	Y *(F)*	Y
Glossop Borough	1947	–	–
Devonshire County	1966	Y	Y (Torquay 11K/22P★)
Exeter City	1966	Y	Y
Plymouth City Borough until 1928	1967	Y	Y 47 K/P
Tiverton Borough	1943	–	–
Dorsetshire County	1967	–	Y (Poole 14K/16P)
Durham County	–	Y	Y
Gateshead County Borough	1968	Y	Y – 16K
Hartlepool Borough	1947	–	–
South Shields County Borough	1968	Y	Y – 25K/18P
Sunderland County Borough	1967	Y	Y – 37K/2P
Essex County	1969	–	–
Colchester Borough	1947	–	–
Southend-on-Sea County Borough	1969	Y *(F)*	–
Gloucestershire County	–	Y	–
Bristol City	1974	–	Y
Hampshire County	1943	–	Y (Bournemouth)
Isle of Wight	1943	–	–
Portsmouth City	1967	Y *(F)*	Y – 37P★
Southampton County Borough	1967	–	Y (in 1942)
Winchester City	1943	Y	–

Police Force	Year of Initial Merger, Renaming or Amalgamation of a Force after 1923 #	Adopted or Proposed a Police Box System between 1923 & 1931 +	Adopted or Proposed a GPO PA1 Call System between 1932 & 1939 + K=Kiosk, P=Pillar
ENGLAND			
Herefordshire County	1967	–	–
Hereford City	1947	–	Y
Hertfordshire County	–	–	–
St Albans City	1947	–	Y
Huntingdonshire County	1965	–	–
Kent County	–	–	–
Canterbury City	1943	–	–
Dover Borough	1943	–	–
Folkestone Borough	1943	–	Y – 5K/12P
Gravesend Borough	1943	Y	Y
Maidstone Borough	1943	–	Y – 4K/32P
Margate Borough	1943	–	Y – 10K/22P
Ramsgate Borough	1943	–	Y – 13P★
Rochester City	1943	–	Y – 2K/25P
Tunbridge Wells Borough	1943	–	Y
Lancashire County	–	–	Y (Seaforth, Denton, Stretford)
Accrington Borough	1947	–	Y – 17 P
Ashton-under-Lyne Borough	1947	Y	–
Bacup Borough	1947	–	Y
Barrow in Furness County Borough	1969	–	–
Blackburn County Borough	1969	–	Y
Blackpool County Borough	1969	–	Y
Bolton County Borough	1969	–	Y – 78 P
Bootle County Borough	1967	–	Y
Burnley County Borough	1969	Y	–
Clitheroe Borough	1947	–	–
Lancaster City	1947	Y	Y – 4K/12P
Liverpool City	1967	Y	–
Manchester City	1968	Y	Y – 86K
Oldham County Borough	1969	Y *(F)*	–

Police Force	Year of Initial Merger, Renaming or Amalgamation of a Force after 1923 #	Adopted or Proposed a Police Box System between 1923 & 1931 +	Adopted or Proposed a GPO PA1 Call System between 1932 & 1939 + K=Kiosk, P=Pillar
ENGLAND			
Preston County Borough	1969	–	Y
Rochdale County Borough	1969	Y	Y
St Helens County Borough	1969	Y	Y
Salford City	1968	Y	–
Southport County Borough	1969	–	–
Warrington County Borough	1969	–	Y (in 1940)
Wigan County Borough	1969	Y	Y (in 1940)
Leicestershire County	1951	Y	–
Leicester City	1967	Y	Y – 39K/6P
Lincolnshire County	–	Y	Y
Boston Borough	1947	–	–
Grantham Borough	1947	–	–
Great Grimsby County Borough	1967	Y	Y
Lincoln City	1967	–	Y
(London)			
Metropolitan		Y	–
City of London		Y	–
Monmouthshire County	1967	–	–
Newport County Borough	1967	Y★	Y
Norfolk County	1968	–	–
Great Yarmouth County Borough	1968	Y	–
King's Lynn Borough	1947	–	–
Norwich City	1968	Y	–
Northamptonshire County	1966	–	Y (Kettering)
Liberty of Peterborough	1947	–	–
Northampton County Borough	1966	Y	Y
Peterborough City	1947	–	Y
Northumberland County	1974	–	–
Newcastle upon Tyne City	1969	Y	–
Tynemouth County Borough	1969	Y	Y – 20K/5P
Nottinghamshire County	1968	–	–

Police Force	Year of Initial Merger, Renaming or Amalgamation of a Force after 1923 [#]	Adopted or Proposed a Police Box System between 1923 & 1931 [+]	Adopted or Proposed a GPO PA1 Call System between 1932 & 1939 [+] K=Kiosk, P=Pillar
ENGLAND			
Newark Borough	1947	–	Y
Nottingham City	1968	Y *(F[1])*	–
Oxfordshire County	1968	–	–
Banbury Borough	1925	–	–
Oxford City	1968	–	Y
Rutland County	1951	–	–
Shropshire County	1967	–	–
Shrewsbury Borough	1947	Y	–
Somersetshire County	1967	–	–
Bath City	1967	Y *(F)*	–
Bridgwater Borough	1940	–	Y – 14P★
Staffordshire County	1968	–	Y
Newcastle under Lyme Borough	1947	–	Y – 36P
Stoke on Trent City	1968	–	Y
Walsall County Borough	1966	–	Y – 17K/6P★
Wolverhampton County Borough	1966	Y *(F)*	Y – 1K/54P★
East Suffolk County	1967	–	–
Ipswich County Borough	1967	Y	–
West Suffolk County	1967	–	–
Surrey County	–	–	–
Guildford Borough	1943	–	–
Reigate Borough	1943	–	Y – 22P★
East Sussex County	1943	–	–
Brighton County Borough	1943	Y	Y
Eastbourne County Borough	1943	Y	Y – 16K/16P
Hastings and St Leonard's on Sea County Borough	1943	Y	Y
Hove Borough	1943	Y	–
West Sussex County	1943	–	–
Warwickshire County	1969	–	–
Birmingham City	1974	Y *(F)*	Y

Police Force	Year of Initial Merger, Renaming or Amalgamation of a Force after 1923 #	Adopted or Proposed a Police Box System between 1923 & 1931+	Adopted or Proposed a GPO PA1 Call System between 1932 & 1939+ K=Kiosk, P=Pillar
ENGLAND			
Coventry City	1969	Y	–
Leamington Spa Borough	1947	–	Y (in 1941)
Westmorland County	1963	–	–
Kendal Borough	1947	–	–
Wiltshire County	–	–	–
Salisbury City	1943	–	Y
Worcestershire County	1967	–	–
Dudley County Borough	1966	Y	Y – 15K/1P★
Kidderminster Borough	1947	Y	–
Worcester City	1967	Y	Y
East Riding of Yorkshire	1968	–	–
Beverley Borough	1928	–	–
Kingston upon Hull City	1974	Y	–
North Riding of Yorkshire	1968	–	–
Middlesbrough County Borough	1968	Y	Y – 26K★
Scarborough Borough	1947	–	–
West Riding of Yorkshire	1968	–	–
Barnsley County Borough	1968	Y	Y
Bradford City	1974	Y	Y
Dewsbury County Borough	1968	Y	–
Doncaster County Borough	1968	Y	Y – 6K/28P
Halifax County Borough	1968	Y *(F²)*	–
Huddersfield County Borough	1968	Y	Y – 37K/P
Leeds City	1974	Y	Y
Rotherham County Borough	1967	–	Y – 18K/7P
Sheffield City	1967	Y	Y – 150K★
Wakefield City	1968	Y	Y
York City	1968	Y	Y – 16K/4P
WALES			
Anglesey County	1950	–	–
Breconshire County	1948	–	–

Police Force	Year of Initial Merger, Renaming or Amalgamation of a Force after 1923#	Adopted or Proposed a Police Box System between 1923 & 1931+	Adopted or Proposed a GPO PA1 Call System between 1932 & 1939+ K=Kiosk, P=Pillar
WALES			
Caernarvonshire County	1950	–	–
Cardiganshire County	1958	–	–
Carmarthenshire County	1958	–	–
Carmarthen Borough	1944	–	–
Denbighshire County	1967	–	–
Flintshire County	1967	–	–
Glamorganshire County	1969	–	–
Cardiff City	1969	Y *(F)*	–
Merthyr Tydfil County Borough	1969	–	–
Neath Borough	1947	–	–
Swansea County Borough	1969	Y	–
Merionethshire County	1950	–	–
Montgomeryshire County	1948	–	–
Pembrokeshire County	1968	–	–
Radnorshire County	1948	–	–
SCOTLAND			
Aberdeenshire County	1949	–	–
Aberdeen City	1975	Y	Y
Angus County	1928–1975	–	–
Arbroath Burgh	1949	–	–
Brechin City	1930	–	–
Dundee City	1975	Y *(F)*	Y
Forfar Burgh	1930	–	–
Montrose Burgh	1930	–	–
Argyllshire County	1975	–	–
Ayrshire County	1975	–	–
Ayr Burgh	1968	Y	Y – 22K★
Kilmarnock Burgh	1968	–	Y – 1K/16P★
Banffshire County	1949	–	–
Berwickshire County	1948	–	–
Buteshire County	1949	–	–

Police Force	Year of Initial Merger, Renaming or Amalgamation of a Force after 1923 #	Adopted or Proposed a Police Box System between 1923 & 1931+	Adopted or Proposed a GPO PA1 Call System between 1932 & 1939+ K=Kiosk, P=Pillar
SCOTLAND			
Rothesay Burgh	1923	–	–
Caithness-shire County	1969	–	–
Clackmannanshire County	1949	–	–
Alloa Burgh	1930	–	–
Dunbartonshire County	1975	–	Y (Clydebank)
Dumbarton Burgh	1949	–	–
Dumfries-shire County	1948	–	–
Dumfries Burgh	1932	–	–
East Lothian County	1950	–	–
Fife County	–	–	–
Dunfermline City	1949	–	–
Kirkcaldy Burgh	1949	–	Y
Forfarshire County	1928	–	–
Inverness-shire County	1968	–	–
Inverness Burgh	1968	–	–
Kincardineshire County	1949	–	–
Kinross-shire County	1930	–	–
Kirkcudbrightshire County	1948	–	–
Lanarkshire County	1975	–	–
Airdrie Burgh	1967	–	Y
Coatbridge Burgh	1967	–	Y
Glasgow City	1975	Y	Y
Hamilton Burgh	1949	Y	–
Motherwell and Wishaw Burgh	1930–1967	–	Y
Midlothian County	1950	–	–
Edinburgh City	1975	Y (F³)	Y
Morayshire County	1930	–	–
Nairnshire County	1930	–	–
Orkney County	1969	–	–
Peebles-shire County	1950	–	–
Perthshire County	1930	–	–
Perth City	1964	–	–

Police Force	Year of Initial Merger, Renaming or Amalgamation of a Force after 1923 #	Adopted or Proposed a Police Box System between 1923 & 1931 +	Adopted or Proposed a GPO PA1 Call System between 1932 & 1939 + K=Kiosk, P=Pillar
SCOTLAND			
Renfrewshire County	1949		Y (Giffnock)
Greenock Burgh	1967	Y	Y – 34K/P
Johnstone Burgh	1930	Y (post merge)	–
Paisley Burgh	1967	Y	Y – 32K★
Renfrew Burgh	1930	Y (post merge)	Y
Ross and Cromarty County	1963	–	–
Roxburghshire County	1948	–	–
Hawick Burgh	1930	–	–
Selkirkshire County	1948	–	–
Galashiels Burgh	1930	–	–
Stirlingshire County	1949	–	–
Stirling Burgh	1938	–	–
Sutherlandshire County	1963	–	–
West Lothian County	1950	–	–
Wigtownshire County	1948	–	–
Zetland County	1969	–	–
Lerwick Burgh	1940	–	–
NORTHERN IRELAND			
Royal Ulster Constabulary	2001	–	–
ISLE OF MAN			
Isle of Man Constabulary	–	–	Y (Douglas)
CHANNEL ISLANDS			
Guernsey Island Police	–	–	–
St Helier Paid Police – Jersey	1952	–	–

Those shown above in italics, in respect of England (apart from London), Wales and Scotland are the County Constabularies under which are listed the borough, county borough and city forces falling within their boundaries or associated with them.

\#   At a later date some forces reverted to their original status and name *e.g.* Brighton County Borough became part of Sussex Combined in 1943 and resumed its original position in 1947. Similarly some counties subsequently reverted to their original name, *e.g.* Bedfordshire renamed Bedfordshire and Luton only between 1966 and 1974.

\+   These early schemes have, in some cases, been recorded from limited references on official documents and actual implementation of a few could not be confirmed. More research will undoubtedly identify other systems, not shown on the list, that were installed within the period.

★   Installation not confirmed and may not have proceeded beyond the planning stage or the numbers quoted could have been changed before installation.

(F) The facility used jointly with another authority usually the fire brigade.

(F¹) Nottingham City Police had a few timber kiosks in addition to the use of fire telephones.

(F²) Halifax County Borough Police jointly used call points on tramway routes.

(F³) Edinburgh City Police had used fire telephones but were in the process of introducing a major police box system.

APPENDIX B

Police Box Memories
Some Personal Recollections

Most policemen who served up to the 1960s will have good and bad memories of police boxes. Throughout the chapters recollections of policemen about specific incidents they encountered have been used as illustrations to, hopefully, breathe some life, into the police box. In this section three retired officers recall the schemes in their particular force.

Tynemouth County Borough Police

Retired Police Constable Bob Walker who served in the Tynemouth Force and subsequently, after amalgamation, the Northumberland Constabulary, has effectively summarised in his account an operational system in a county borough:

"Prior to 1969 the conurbation of Tyneside was policed from the mouth of the river on the north side by the separate Forces of Tynemouth, Northumberland and Newcastle and on the south side by South Shields, Durham and Gateshead. The river came under the jurisdiction of the only independent river police in the United Kingdom, the River Tyne Police. I was in the County Borough of Tynemouth Force and, after the amalgamation, with the Northumberland Constabulary.

Tynemouth and Newcastle adopted very similar Police Box Systems. As the system came into effect Tynemouth closed its sub-stations and for many men the only time they went to the Central Police Station was to collect their pay or if obliged to operationally.

My personal recollections of the system commence in 1946 when the Force area was divided into sixteen beats or patrol areas (by the time of the 1969 amalgamations they had been increased to twenty-two). Each beat had its Beat Box with the beats so planned that a constable on one beat could have access to as many as four boxes when on patrol. In addition there were 'spare' boxes and telephone standards for use. The public had direct speech contact to the Central Police Station from all boxes and pillars.

The green painted Beat Boxes had been constructed to a standard design in wood with a sloping roof. At the highest point a lamp, coloured blue or orange, could be operated to 'flash' by the control room using the direct telephone line. Inside the box was coat hangers, shelves, a small desk type table with a drawer and a stool.

All types of forms were kept in the box for use by the constable and a ledger sized notebook, known as a 'Rough Book', was retained for noting matters requiring attention. Standing Orders and Photographic Circulars of wanted persons were frequently pinned to the back of the box. Beneath the telephone cabinet was another cupboard, with access from inside and outside the box, which contained a metal box of first aid equipment. Wooden splints were kept inside the box accessible only to the constable.

Access to the public emergency telephone was gained by opening a metal door to the cabinet bearing the words – POLICE. FIRE. AMBULANCE. When this door was opened fully the roof lamp of the box illuminated permanently, to draw a patrolling constable's attention to the box, and a red light appeared on the Central Police Station switchboard. The user, upon opening the door, spoke into a metal grille through which he received a reply. Closing the door, which had a fairly strong spring hinge, automatically extinguished the box roof light.

Beats varied in size according to the population and property density. A cycle was used on large beats on the outskirts, and the Beat Box had a cycle shed alongside usually capable of holding two cycles. Refreshments (sandwiches and a flask) were taken in the Beat Box at a specified time and there was a small brush for the night shift man to sweep it out. A single electric light illuminated a box and in some there was a small electric fire. The 'spare' boxes were identical to the Beat Boxes except that they did not have a 'Rough Book' and invariably less paper work.

During World War Two the boxes were encased in sandbags and concrete with a protective shield of sandbags in the front. At least three were destroyed by enemy action and one received a direct hit from a bomb killing and injuring occupants.
Standards were rented from the G.P.O. and positioned in the shopping area of the town.

In the late 1940s three of the wooden boxes were replaced by ones of brick construction, about ten feet square, but with the same facilities as those they replaced, except more room. In the mid-1950s three more wooden boxes were replaced by 'section houses' and others, through deterioration, by new wooden boxes with flat roofs. The public gained access from the outside to the same telephone as the constable used inside. These boxes were painted yellow.

The Section Houses were brick built like a small chalet. They comprised of a room, similar to that in the first brick boxes, with a door leading to a hallway from which another door led to separate toilet and washroom facilities. There was also a door into a kitchen type room with gas cooker, hot water geyser, sink, worktop and cupboards and drawers. Incorporated too was a cycle cupboard with access only from the outside. These 'Houses', although principally 'Beat Boxes', were used as starting points for constables on adjacent beats and for refreshment periods."

Stockport County Borough Police

Stockport was another town to adopt a police box system in the early 1920s. Although early records of this system have not been located Police Constable Roy Stafford, who served in the force in the 1960s (retired as an Inspector in the Metropolitan Police), amusingly recollects policing with boxes in a small county borough:

"I do remember that they were built of white precast concrete about four to five feet square and narrowing towards the top and with a white light at the pinnacle. A little red door gave access to the phone and the box was furnished with a table and stool.

There weren't that many really in the town of about 36 square miles. The whole was divided into 25 beats but I can picture only eight boxes at the most remote locations.

The box was home to an official police bike. This was 'prehistoric' having 28 inch wheels with corresponding frame size. It was designed for the more acceptable size constable of the day not I who was acknowledged to be the shortest person in the force. In fact it wasn't suitable for many and we all had our own (no allowance payable). It was accordingly not uncommon for two bikes to be entwined in the box thus making any efforts to sleep in the box on nights difficult.

It was normal to visit the box every hour at fixed times and complete an entry in a route book for the ensuing hour and ring in.

The patrolling Sergeant (rarely the Inspector unless he was being driven) would hope to locate you on that route or, if feeling perverse, catch you idling in the box either before or after the appropriate time. Some of the more astute Sergeants would arrange a meet. This was advantageous to both parties as it was not unusual for the Sergeant to miss you on your 'round' and become frustrated by the time he found you. There were very valid reasons for missing each other, but Sergeants never seemed to appreciate the fact which was odd really since they'd all been P.C.s in the borough and 'watering holes' didn't change that much. I must confess I think sometimes this was turned into a game of hide and seek.

Also retained in the box were the beat cards and vulnerable premises cards. There were dozens of these especially during the holidays. Many of the populace advised police of their absence and the P.C. was expected to visit at least once during his tour and note the time on the card. Really clever Sergeants could sometimes deduce that your prescribed route and time on a card did not gel. This made him very smug and proved that the P.C. would not be C.I.D. material.

There were long termers cards – years – who left a flask of tea out for the night man. These were really clever because you had to attend in order to dispose of the tea – no false entry possible here.

Sometimes the box had to accommodate prisoners waiting for a ride. That was of course in the days when the apprehended villain would walk with you back to the box – often a considerable distance. In this connection I have heard of prisoners being incarcerated in a box whilst the 'hero' went in search of the accomplice – did that really happen?

There was also the case of the officer who not liking the dark managed never to leave the vicinity of the box between rings.

I suppose, on reflection, a Police Box was quite a friendly place. I've never considered it before. It was a haven from the elements, a point of contact, meeting place, bike shed, cell, office, canteen, smoke room, animal shelter (never a study, like those in the Met). It was probably used as a place of ill repute by some of the characters I knew if one can believe rumour.

Not bad for a little box.

The box was of course primarily for the benefit of the general populace in the days before Mr Bell made his mark on every household. They had immediate contact with their emergency services and they always knew where to find a copper even if they couldn't pinpoint the precise time and most probably knew that also. Even the white light had its uses because once it was flashing for attention some nosey parker was bound to inform you.

How much more can you say about a simple, now extinct, Police Box."

Winchester City Police

Police Constable Richard Day joined the Winchester City Police in June 1934, and retired in 1959, by which time the Force had been amalgamated into the Hampshire County Constabulary. P.C. Day provides a valuable insight into a relatively small city system in Winchester:

"I joined the Winchester City Police in June 1934. There were eight large boxes and five smaller ones, all situated in various parts of the City, and identified by number, Box 1, Box 2 and so on.

The large boxes were constructed of concrete, and of a size to accommodate two people. The box had a telephone with direct line to the Police Station, and it could also be used by members of the public via a small door situated on the side of the box. There was a bench, a large book for recording messages received from the Police Station, and times etc. of visits made. There was also a small one bar electric fire. Copies of daily information and other Police literature were also kept in them. A large wooden stool was also provided. Needless to say boxes were not built for comfort although Police Officers on their particular beats had to use them to partake of food and drink for the half hour break that was the regulation at that time.

The smaller boxes containing only a telephone were situated either on walls or telephone poles.

At that particular time in the history of the Police and its workings, boxes served a useful purpose as regular visits were made at times to phone to the Police Station. Information concerning local crime, persons wanted, Express Messages etc. were received and recorded. Officers when calling to the Police Station would often be despatched to the scene of accidents, sudden deaths, traffic congestion and other incidents.

During the war sandbags protected the boxes, as they were used as assembly points for regular officers, and Special Constables during air raid warning periods. We were amalgamated fairly early in the war with the Hampshire Force and the Isle of Wight Force. The boxes continued in use as before but gradual changes began to be made. The beat system was altered whereby all officers worked from the Police Station and not from the boxes, although they were still used for making contact. No meals were taken in them, and when the refreshment period was extended to ¾ of an hour the day duty officers were allowed to go home, and the night duty shift used the parade room at the Station.

At the time of my retirement in 1959 the boxes were still being used, but on a much more limited scale. With the introduction of personal hand sets the large boxes were demolished and the smaller ones were removed."

APPENDIX C

Some Locations of Surviving Police Kiosks (+) and Pillars (#)

Museums and Police Premises

Amberley Working Museum, West Sussex		#
Avoncroft Museum of Buildings, Bromsgrove	+	#
City of London Police Museum		#
Coventry Transport Museum	+	
Glasgow Police Museum	+	
Grampian Transport Museum, Alford	+	
Galleries of Justice, Nottingham	+	
Kent Police Museum, Chatham Historic Dockyard	+	#
Leicestershire Constabulary Headquarters		#
Museum of Transport, Glasgow	+	
Metropolitan Police Historical Collection, Empress State Building		#
Metropolitan Police Motor Collection, Hampton		#
Metropolitan Police Station, Northwood		#
Metropolitan Police Training School, Hendon	+	#
National Tramway Museum, Crich, Derbyshire	+	#
Nottinghamshire Police Headquarters	+	
Police Staff College, Bramshill†		#
Ripon Prison and Police Museum, North Yorkshire		#
Rochester Police Station, Kent		#
Thames Valley Police Museum, Sulhamstead		#
West Yorkshire Police Training Centre, Bishopgarth, Wakefield	+	

Public Places

Brighton	Outside Palace Pier (Sandwich Bar)	+
Eastbourne	Albert Parade (brick structure)	+
	Green Street, between public toilets (brick structure)	+
	Seaside, in front of municipal baths (brick structure)	+

Edinburgh (Not all locations verified. Hopefully none are duplicated)

Bruntsfield Place	+	
Canongate	+	(L)
Charterhall Road	+	(L)
Cowgate	+	(L)
Dean Terrace	+	(L)
Drummond Place	+	(L)
Drumsheugh Gardens	+	(L)
Fountainbridge (Coffee Stall)	+	
Gilmerton	+	
Grassmarket (ex-Police Information Box)	+	(L)
Heriot Row	+	(L)
Hunter Square, High Street (ex-Police Information Box)	+	(L)
Hope Park Crescent (Coffee Stall)	+	
Lauriston Place	+	
Lawnmarket (ex-Police Information Box)	+	(L)
Leith Walk (Coffee Stall)	+	
Little King Street (resited here as Coffee Stall)	+	
Marchmont Crescent	+	
Market Street	+	(L)
Maybury Road	+	
Middle Meadow Walk (Coffee Stall)	+	
Melville Drive	+	
Morningside Road (resited here as Coffee Stall)	+	
Murrayfield Avenue	+	(L)
Newbattle Terrace	+	(L)
St Patrick's Square (Coffee Stall)	+	
Pier Place, Newhaven Harbour	+	(L)
Princes Street, The Mound	+	(L)
Register Place	+	(L)
Richmond Lane	+	
Rose Street (resited here as Coffee Stall)	+	
Rutland Square	+	(L)
Shore	+	(L)
Tollcross	+	
West Port	+	(L)
West Princes Street Gardens	+	(L)
Whitehorse Loan	+	(L)

Glasgow	Buchanan Street	+	(L)
	Cathedral Square	+	(L)
	Great Western Road (Coffee Stall)	+	(L)
	Wilson Street	+	(L)
Huddersfield	Almondbury	+	
Leicestershire	Newtown Linford, entrance to Bradgate Park	+	
London (City Police)	Aldersgate Street, EC		#
	Aldgate High Street, EC		#
	Guildhall Yard, EC		#
	Liverpool Street, EC		#
	Old Broad Street, EC		#
	Queen Victoria Street, EC		#
	Victoria Embankment EC		#
	Walbrook, EC		#
London (Metropolitan)	Grosvenor Square, W1		#
	Piccadilly Circus, W1		#
	Trafalgar Square, W1 (stone structure)	+	
Portsmouth	Eastern Road, Farlington (brick structure)	+	
Scarborough	Sandside	+	
Sheffield	Outside the Town Hall	+	
Newport, Gwent	Somerton Crescent	+	

Other brick built structures have probably survived elsewhere and are in use for other purposes. A few wooden boxes may have survived as garden sheds, etc.

(L) *Listed by Historic Scotland.*

† *Presented to the College in 1987 by the UK Atomic Energy Authority Constabulary.*

GENERAL READING AND REFERENCES

Bunker, John, From Rattle to Radio. Brewin Books, 1988

Cockcroft, W. R., From Cutlasses to Computers – The Police Force in Liverpool, 1836–1989. S.B. Publications, 1991

Critchley, T. A., A History of Police in England and Wales. Constable, 1967

Grant, Douglas, The Thin Blue Line – The Story of the Glasgow City Police. Long, 1973

Hutchings, Walter, Out of the Blue: History of the Devon Constabulary. Devonshire Press, 1957

Ingleton, Roy, Policing Kent. Phillimore, 2002

Irvine, Hamish, The Diced Cap: The Story of Aberdeen City Police. Police, 1972

Jacobs, Leslie C., Constables of Suffolk – A Brief History of Policing in the County. Suffolk Constabulary, 1992

Johannessen, Neil, Telephone Boxes, Shire Publications, 1988

Madigan, T. S., The Men Who Wore Straw Helmets: Policing in Luton, 1840–1974. Book Castle, 1993

Povey, P. J. *and* Earl, R. A. J., Vintage Telephones of the World. Peter Peregrinus, 1988

Ripley, Howard, Police Forces of Great Britain and Ireland – their Amalgamations and their Buttons. Hazell, 1983

Sillitoe, Sir Percy, Cloak Without Dagger. Cassell, 1955

Smith, Gordon, Bradford's Police. Bradford City Police, 1974

Stallion, Martin & Wall, David S., The British Police. Police Forces and Chief Officers 1829–2000. Police History Society, 1999

Stafford, Robert, Lost Property – Police Boxes and Cabmen's Shelters of Hull. Local History Unit, Hull College, 1998

Stamp, Gavin, Telephone Boxes. Chatto & Windus, 1989

Thompson, S.P., Maintaining the Queen's Peace. A Short History of the Birkenhead Borough Police. The Force, 1958

Tunstall, Alf *and* Cowdell, Jeff, Policing the Potteries. Three Counties Publishing, 2002

Articles in Periodicals, Journals etc.

PRPG – Police Review & Parade Gossip (renamed Police Review in June, 1930)

Electric Police Signal Systems *The Times*, 24 July, 1889

Friederici, Otto, A paper headed – Electrical Appliances – *To the Civil and Mechanical Engineers' Society*, 1891

Pocket Telephones for Police – Newcastle *PRPG*, 10 April, 1893

A New Police Signal System – Liverpool *PRPG*, 5 January, 1894

Police Signalling in Liverpool, *PRPG,* 6 March 1896

Sales Catalogue *The National Telephone Co. Ltd*, 1903

Sales Catalogue *Western Electric Company*, 1908/1909

Owen, W. C., Fire Alarm System at Bath *The National Telephone Journal*, July, 1909

The Sunderland Scheme – Chief Constable's Report to the Town Council *PRPG*, 22 June, 1923

Leeds Police Fire Brigade *PRPG*, 19 October, 1923

Police Fire Alarm – Southend on Sea First Town to Adopt Latest System *PRPG*, 11 January, 1924

Wolverhampton Borough – Installation of Police, Ambulance and Fire Alarm System *PRPG*, 14 January, 1924

Sunderland Police Ambulance and Call-Box System *PRPG*, 8 February, 1924

Sunderland Police Box System – Extract from the Chief Constable's Annual Report *PRPG*, 21 March, 1924

Police Box System – Tynemouth *PRPG*, 6 February, 1925

Police Box System – Burnley *PRPG*, 3 July, 1925

Police Box System – Burnley *PRPG*, 16 October, 1925

Police Box System – The Exeter Arrangements *PRPG*, 24 December, 1925

Pill Boxes – Memphis, Tennessee – *PRPG*, January, 1926

Street Telephone Signals – Unique System in Halifax *PRPG*, 8 January, 1926

Reorganisation of Newcastle on Tyne Force *PRPG*, 26 February, 1926

Police Box System – Wolverhampton *PRPG*, 12 March, 1926

Nicholson, A. F., Chief Constable of Exeter Police Telephone Boxes *PRPG*, 19 March, 1926

Glasgow Police Reorganisation *Glasgow Herald*, 12 June 1926

Telephone Box System – Criticism of the Devon Arrangements *PRPG*, 16 July, 1926

Police Telephone Boxes – Contribution from a Ranker, Devon *PRPG*, 20 August, 1926

Telephone Box System – Derby Scheme claimed to be 'First in Britain' *PRPG*, 1 October, 1926

Police Boxes – Great Grimsby *PRPG*, 8 April 1927

Police Boxes – Middlesbrough *PRPG*, 8 April 1927

Police Box System – Eastbourne Station to be closed *PRPG*, 22 July, 1927

Burnley's Phone Box System *PRPG*, 26 August, 1927

The 'Carter-Micro' Police Kiosk and Pillar *Sales Brochure Carter & Co. (Nelson) Ltd.*, 1927

The Sheffield Police Boxes *The Telegraph & Telephone Journal*, January, 1928

Southend and Portsmouth System *Sporting Times*, 22 December, 1928

Manchester's Police Box System *PRPG*, ?, 1928

Crawley, Frederick, Decentralisation and the Police Box System Newcastle upon Tyne *Police Journal*, Vol. 1, 1928

Winchester's Police Box System *PRPG*, 26 July, 1929

Police Boxes – Experimental Trial at Leeds *PRPG*, 18 October, 1929

Introduction of the Metropolitan Police Box System Articles in *various newspapers* on 29/30 November, 1929

Police Box System – First Section of Metro Area Opened *PRPG*, 6 December, 1929

Crawley, F. J., The Police Box System *Safety First*, April 1930

The Public and Police Call Boxes – Wigan *PRPG*, 13 June, 1930

Police Efficiency – Salford's New Signal Device *Manchester Guardian*, 24 September, 1930

Police Boxes – New Design for South Shields *PRPG*, 17 October, 1930

Police Boxes – New Leeds Police Notes – Box with a Powerful Long Distance Lamp *PRPG*, 24 October, 1930

Modified Police Box System *PRPG*, 6 March, 1931

Police Box Switchboard Attendants, Leicestershire *PRPG*, 2 April, 1931

Rural Police Box System *PRPG*, 22 May, 1931

Wayside Boxes *Architects Journal*, 30 September, 1931

Simon, L., Possibilities for the Telegraph Telephone and Teleprinter Service as affecting the Police and Fire Brigades – Address by L. Simon of the G.P.O. to the Chief Constables' Association *PRPG*, l5 July, 1932

Police Telephones and Signals – A New System *Ericsson Bulletin*, January, 1933

New Boxes at Wolverhampton *Police Chronicle*, 28 April, 1933

Edinburgh Police Box System – A New Era *Police Chronicle*, 9 June, 1933

Police Boxes – Inauguration in Edinburgh *PRPG*, 9 June, 1933

Planning of Police Communications *Ericsson Bulletin*, July, 1933

Pillar Street Telephones at Birmingham *Police Chronicle*, 22 September, 1933

Steel Dundee Boxes *PRPG*, 29 September, 1933

Success of Police Box System – Blackburn *PRPG*, 16 February, 1934

Wood v Concrete – Salford *PRPG*, 23 March, 1934

Up to Date Police Boxes – Reading Borough Police *PRPG*, 29 March, 1934

Norwich Police Boxes *PRPG*, 22 June, 1934

Public Utility Boxes – Chief Constable's Scheme *Daily Telegraph*, 5 September, 1934

Police Told to Move their Police Box *Evening News*, 11 September, 1934

Police Phone Moved Off *Daily Sketch*, 12 September, 1934

The Police Box in Rural Areas – The Advantages and Disadvantages of the System – Article by a Leicestershire Police Constable *The Police Journal*, Vol. VIII, 1935

Gateshead Install Latest Kiosks *PRPG*, 4 January, 1935

Brighton's Improved Telephone System *PRPG*, 16 August, 1935

New Telephone System at St Albans *PRPG*, 13 September, 1935

A Fifty Year Old Police Box – Greenock *PRPRG,* 16 October, 1936

Police Box System – Brighton *PRPG*, 18 February, 1937

Post Office *Telephone Sales Bulletin* Volume 3, No. 7, July, 1937

Morris, T. G., Police Telephone Systems *Post Office Electrical Engineers Journal*, October, 1937

Pillar Telephones at Accrington *PRPG*, 24 December, 1937

Wright, C. H., The London Fire Brigade Alarm System *Post Office Electrical Engineers Journal*, Vol. 30, January, 1938

Wales and Border Counties New Police Telephone and Signal System *Post Office Electrical Engineers Journal*, Vol. 47, April, 1954

Porritt, W. R., A New Police Telephone and Signalling System *Post Office Electrical Engineers Journal*, Vol. 49, April, 1956

Peter's Police Posts *The Job*, 30 June, 1972

Farewell to the Old Blue Police Boxes *City Recorder*, 7 April, 1988

Stewart, Dr. Robert W. & Carmichael, Fiona, The Police Signal Box in Glasgow – A Short History *Strathclyde Guardian*, Vol. 17, No. 3, September, 1993

Goodbye to All This *The Job (Metropolitan Police Newspaper)* 26 September, 1969

Stewart, Dr. Robert W., The Police Signal Box – A 100 Year History *Engineering and Education Journal*, August, 1994

Bunker, John, Bunker on Boxes *London Police Pensioner*, No. 78, September, 1995

Howard, R., Tardis – Police Telephone Boxes, Sheffield *Police History Society Journal* No. 5, 1999

Croxson, Ernie, If You Want to Know the Time – Pre-War Policing in Norwich *Police History Society Journal*, 2000

Race on to Save Police Relic *The Coventry Observer*, 26 March, 2004

Appleby, Roger, To Meet the Requirements of the City – publication and date unknown

Police Signalling Apparatus – *Siemens Brothers & Co. Ltd.*, London – undated

Fire Alarm Telegraphs – *Descriptive Pamphlet – Single-Wire Multiple Telephone Signal Company Limited* (Saunders and Brown System) – undated

Public Fire Alarms Police and Ambulance Calls (Moore and Knight Systems) *Sales Catalogue – Walters Electrical Manufacturing Co. Ltd, London* – undated

Sales Catalogue *Boulton & Paul Ltd., Norwich* – undated

Sutcliffe, Jack, An Old Friend *Patrol: Journal of the Bradford City Police* – date unknown

Police and Constabulary Almanac, various issues

History leaflets of the various merged borough forces *West Yorkshire Police*

Other Sources

A major part of the research for this book was carried out at the Public Record Office (now The National Archives), Kew, the Post Office Archives, the British Telecom Technology Showcase, Blackfriars (now closed) and the British Telecom Museum, Oxford (now closed). The BT Archive, High Holborn now hold documents previously held elsewhere. Although I have not attempted to list all my sources of information below are some that may be of interest to the researcher –

National Archive and BT Archived Files

Various Forces' Boxes and Information	H045/16973
Police Box Information	H045/17006
Newcastle & Sunderland Boxes	H045/22811
Various Box Information	H045/23137
Telegraphs to Met Fixed Points	POST30/225B
Police Box Systems / Details of Met System	POST33/3415
Met. Police System	POST33/3416
Rochester Police	POST33/3955
Leeds and Rochdale Police	POST33/4571
Director of Telegraphs and Telephone Conference	POST33/5260
Various Post Office Research Reports	TCB22/
Metropolitan Police Boxes	MEP02/359
Metropolitan Police Boxes	MEP02/2576
Metropolitan Fixed Point Boxes	MEP02/8827
Metropolitan Police Boxes	MEP02/9488
Metropolitan Police Boxes	MEP02/10607
Islington and Brixton Boxes	MEP05/72
Metropolitan Fixed Point Boxes	MEP05/86
Metropolitan Fixed Point Boxes	MEP05/87
Metropolitan Police Boxes	MEP05/347

Official Documents

Post Office Telegraphs – Private Wire Estimate No. 182, 17 October, 1871

Fire Brigade Stations to which Call Points are connected – Metropolitan Police Orders, 18 May, 1880

Telephones and Telegraphs and Municipal Electric Fire Alarms and Police Patrol Signaling Systems – Department of Commerce USA, 1912

Sunderland Borough Police – A Review of the Sunderland Police Box System, 1924

Newcastle City Police – Police Box System as applied to the City of Newcastle upon Tyne, 1926

Middlesbrough Police – Riches, H. Memorandum relating to the Police

Telephone Box System as applied to Middlesbrough, 1 September, 1929

Manchester City Police – Extract from the Handbook, 1929

Hull City – Watch and Licensing Committee Minutes 1930-1932

Glasgow, City of, – Criminal Returns, 1931

G.P.O. – Police Telephone and Signal System, May 1932

G.P.O. – Post Office Standard Police Kiosk and Pillar System,. January, 1933

G.P.O. – Police, Fire and Ambulance Kiosk or Pillar Telephone System, June, 1936

G.P.O. Post Office Telephones – How to Use the Police Telephone and Signal System (Type PA150), 1936

G.P.O. Post Office Telephones – Police, Fire and Ambulance Kiosk or Pillar Telephone System, September, 1938

Southampton Police – Telecommunications System Booklet, 1943

G.P.O. – Circular C66/53 Introduction of New Police Street Call Point System Type PA450, 23 July, 1953

P.O. Engineering Dept. – Engineering Instructions Police Telephone & Signal System PA450, November, 1958

Cambridgeshire Constabulary – Official files on police boxes

Devon and Cornwall Constabulary – Official files on police boxes

Lancashire Constabulary – Archived papers on Blackburn police boxes

Metropolitan Police – Beat Books and Ringing in Schedules

Metropolitan Police – Commissioner's Annual Reports

Metropolitan Police – Museum Box Files

Strathclyde Police – Archived papers on police boxes

Tynemouth Police – Ringing in Schedule

Websites of Interest
Bob's Telephone File

Civil Defence and Emergency Service Preservation Trust

Crich Tramway Museum Restoration of Police Box

Edinburgh Police Boxes

Glasgow's Police Boxes

History of the District of Columbia Fire and Police Call Boxes

Kent Police Museum

Kiosk Korner

Model Police Box Collector – www.policeboxes.com

Newport Police Box

Peter Darrington's Police Box Website

Robert Ore's Kiosk Site – www.redphone.info

Unicorn Restorations

INDEX

Boroughs and county boroughs are indexed as boroughs. Fire alarms and General Post Office, which appear frequently, have not been indexed. Police forces, appearing in the main text, are indexed but not individual towns falling within force areas. Tables at Appendix A and C contain police forces that may not appear in this index.